DATE DUE

DEMCO 38-296

Essential ATM Standards: RFCs and Protocols Made Practical

Other Works in This Series

Pete Loshin, *Essential Email Standards: RFCs and Protocols Made Practical*

Pete Loshin, *Essential Ethernet Standards: RFCs and Protocols Made Practical*

Essential ATM Standards: RFCs and Protocols Made Practical

Pete Loshin

Wiley Computer Publishing

John Wiley & Sons, Inc.

NEW YORK · CHICHESTER · WEINHEIM · BRISBANE · SINGAPORE · TORONTO

n

Electronic Products, Associate Editor: Mike Sosa
Text Design & Composition: Benchmark Productions, Inc.

Library of Congress Cataloging-in-Publication Data:

Loshin, Peter.
  Essential ATM standards: RFCs and protocols made practical/Pete Loshin.
    p. cm.
  ISBN 0-471-34598-9 (cloth : alk. paper)
  1. Asynchronous transfer mode. 2. Internet (Computer network)--Standards.
3. Computer network protocols. I. Title.
TK5105.35.L67   1999
004.6'6--dc21   99-042976
                                                     CIP

Printed in the United States of America.

10 9 8 7 6 5 4 3 2 1

Contents

Acknowledgments

This is where I'd normally ooze thanks effusively, citing the folks at Wiley like Carol Long, Kathryn Malm, and Angela Murphy. Yes, they helped make it happen. But it if weren't for the men and women who have devoted their careers and lives to developing Internet standards, this book—and the Internet itself—would not be possible.

Without those people—anyone who has ever contributed to a workgroup, whether by drafting a document, coding an implementation, submitting an opinion about a specification to workgroup mailing list, or attending an IETF function—none of this would have been possible. I'd like to extend my thanks to each and every one of those people.

Finally, I cannot write an acknowledgment section without mentioning my loving wife, Lisa, and my splendid son, Jacy. And Zoom, for whom we are all eagerly awaiting.

About the Author

Pete Loshin started writing about computers in the late 1980s for *PC Magazine* and *PC Week*, and he shortly afterward discovered TCP/IP and the Internet. Following a six-year stint as a TCP/IP network engineer for an R&D laboratory in Cambridge, MA, Pete began writing full-time. He served as technical editor for *BYTE* Magazine, as well as editor of the newsletter "Corporate Internet Strategies." His articles have appeared in magazines such as *PC World*, *Communications Week*, *Information Security*, *Data Communications*, *Communications News*, *Telecommunications*, and many others. Pete has a bunch of books about TCP/IP, the Internet, and networking, including *TCP/IP Clearly Explained* (Morgan Kaufmann, 1999), *IPv6 Clearly Explained* (Morgan Kaufmann, 1999) and *Extranet Design and Implementation* (SYBEX 1997). Pete expects to have six new titles in print during 1999. You can reach Pete at pete@loshin.com. For more information about Internet standards as well as this and any other book Pete has written, check out www.internet-standard.com.

Introduction

Standards are usually dry, inaccessible (literally and figuratively), and remote from the reality of everyday life. The Internet Request for Comments (RFC) document series includes Internet standards, but more importantly it contains the wit and wisdom of everyone who has helped to make the Internet what it is. Since 1969, engineers and non-engineers have submitted documents to this series, sometimes to document a meeting, sometimes to document a new protocol, sometimes to describe an old problem, sometimes to describe a new approach to solving that problem.

Some RFCs are more important than others, some are easier to read than others. But with the number of RFCs approaching 3,000, the one constant is that when you need to find something out about Internet standards, your best bet is to look for the appropriate RFC. Finding that document may not always be easy, but they're all in there, somewhere.

If only there were somewhere you could turn to get the gist of the standards in some particular arena; email for example, or Ethernet maybe, or even ATM.

That's why I wrote this book. First, so that anyone who needs to know more about Internet standards can find out what they need, no matter what area they are concerned with. And second, so you could have a convenient source that categorizes the standards, summarizes the important ones, and tells you where to look for all the details.

Who Should Read This Book

You need to read this book if you develop Internet applications or any network software or hardware that uses or interfaces with ATM networks. It will help guide you through the salient protocols, and keep you from wasting time looking at the wrong ones.

But you should also read this book if you support Internet protocols over ATM in any way: whether you install software that runs over and hardware that works with ATM or provide technical services to users of such products, understanding how the underlying protocols work will help you do your job better.

If you're involved with network administration, network security, or network design, you should read this book as well. It will help you understand how the relevant Internet protocols work and how you can administer, secure, or design your network with those protocols in mind.

Finally, if you are interested in understanding how the Internet works, whether as a college or graduate student of computer science or simply as a curious person who likes to see how things tick, you should read this book.

What's in This Book

This book is divided into two parts. In the first part, after an introduction to ATM and standards in Chapter 1, we get deep into the Internet standards process. Chapter 2 examines the various Internet standards and non-standards documents and discusses the different classifications that documents can fall into. Chapter 3 introduces the various Internet standards bodies, and related organizations. Chapter 4 covers the process that takes a proposed specification and turns it into a full Internet standard. Chapter 5 offers tips and techniques for locating and downloading exactly the RFC you are looking for, and some pointers to good web sites that can give you more information about RFCs and Internet standards. Chapter 6, gives some pointers to reading and interpreting RFCs. The last chapter in Part One, Chapter 7, provides an overview to the standards related to network management over the Internet and other IP networks.

The first part of the book is the introduction to the world of Internet standards; the rest of the book builds on the information in the first part, taking you through the world of Internet standards for ATM. Chapter 8 provides an overview to ATM itself, while in Chapter 9 we introduce the issues and approaches used for running IP over ATM. In Chapter 10 we cover the IP over ATM (IPOA) approach initially taken by the IETF for running IP over ATM, while in Chapter 11 we look at the ATM Forum's approach to mapping IP (and other network layer protocols) over ATM: LAN Emulation (LANE) and Multiprotocol over ATM (MPOA).

Chapter 12 introduces some of the issues involved in routing IP over ATM, with special attention paid to the Next Hop Resolution Protocol (NHRP). Chapter 13 looks at network traffic management issues, in particular those addressed by resource reservations and quality of service guarantees in both IP and ATM. Chapter 14 discusses ATM network management in the framework of the Simple Network Management Protocol (SNMP) and related Management Information Bases (MIBs). Finally, Chapter 15 discusses some of the work in progress related to ATM standards, and gives some indications of what to expect in the future for ATM and IP standards.

Internet standards continually evolve and develop over time. If something works but could be made to work better, it is likely to eventually be updated. If something doesn't work as it was expected to, it will either be updated so it will work better, or replaced by something that already does work better. This means you've got to be proactive as you study Internet standards--even as you read this book. Most of the material is based on up to date documents and discussion with members of the IETF workgroups responsible for developing new standards. The majority of the material is stable and not expected to be updated any time soon. But that does not mean it won't be updated-- or that it won't be supplemented with new, complementary standards.

If you need to know this stuff, you'll need to know how to keep it all up to date. One way is to subscribe to all the workgroup mailing lists (see chapter 4). Another approach is to check out: http://www.Internet-Standard.com.

This is where you can go to find out the latest about Internet standards as well as get any updates or errata concerning this book. I'll be posting interesting information and news related to standards there, as it comes in.

Finally, the best part of my day is when I receive email from someone who has read one of my books. Whether you like the book or not, whether you found a typo or want to thank me for writing something useful, I welcome all reader email. So just let me know what you think of this book by sending email to me at pete@loshin.com.

I hope you enjoy reading this book as much as I enjoyed writing it.

Internet Standards

Asynchronous Transfer Mode (ATM) was born out of a need for fast, multiplexed, connection-oriented communications pipelines for tele-communications use. As such, it is in many ways antithetical to the world of IP networking, grounded as IP is in a need for connectionless connectivity. The fact that ATM provides a very efficient mechanism for getting bits from one place to another makes it attractive to IP network implementers. The one big thing ATM and IP have in common is their need for open standards.

As long as we adhere to the open standards, we can all get along just fine. The first part of this book builds a foundation for understanding what Internet standards are and how they work. The second part of this book discusses the points at which ATM and Internet standards intersect and how they work together.

Chapter 1, "Internet Standards for ATM," discusses why standards must be defined for IP to work over ATM. Chapter 2, "Internet Standards and Internet Protocols," examines Internet standards and Internet protocols. Chapter 3, "Internet Standards Bodies," explains the organizations involved in creating Internet protocols and setting Internet standards. Chapter 4, "The Internet Standards Process," describes the processes involved in building an Internet standard. Chapter 5, "Getting the RFCs," provides guidance for finding Internet standards as they are described in Request for Comments (RFC) documents, and Chapter 6, "Reading the RFCs," explains how to read and use RFCs. Finally, Chapter 7, "Network Management Fundamentals," provides an overview to the mechanisms used for Internet network management.

Internet Standards for ATM

Getting IP to run over Asynchronous Transfer Mode (ATM) is almost as complicated as converting a diesel locomotive for use on surface streets. ATM has its strengths, and so does IP, but they are very different. IP is great for moving chunks of data around huge heterogeneous networks and leaving the task of routing those chunks of data to the network. ATM is great for moving chunks of data around an ATM network very quickly and without degradation of service even during periods of peak demand. We've included a brief chapter later in the book that provides an overview of the ATM technology (ATM is almost always referred to as a technology, not a protocol), but it is there mostly as a convenience: This book is not about ATM so much as it is about Internet standards for using ATM in IP networks. In this chapter, we discuss why ATM is so important to IP, why it is so difficult, and what the Internet community has done about it.

ATM and IP: Compare and Contrast

Figure 1.1 shows the OSI reference model of internetworking that defines seven different layers at which networks can interoperate. Although the layers can often correspond to actual discernible and discrete functions, they don't have to. Chances are good that you are already familiar with this model as well as with the four-layer Internet Protocol reference model. The thing to remember about this model is that it represents how nodes on a network communicate. The application on a node can interoperate with the application on another node (or even another application on the same node). These applications "connect" at the application layer of whatever network model is being used. Likewise, when a machine is physically attached to the same physical network medium as another machine, they are linked (and interoperate) at the physical layer.

Rather than go into all the details about what each layer means, the OSI reference model is included here to point out that IP (and its related protocols) operates at the higher layers, while ATM operates at the lowest layers. Figure 1.2 shows where IP and ATM usually get mapped on the OSI reference model. Traditionally, ATM is defined as being a mechanism that operates at the physical layer of the protocol stack. However, this description can be confusing. IP sometimes dips down to the data link layer, for example, when an IP node needs to figure out where to send a packet on the local link. ATM reaches up into the data link and even into the network layer at times. For example, while global hierarchical network addressing is usually thought of as a perquisite of the network layer, ATM uses it—and ATM operates at the physical layer, right?

| Application |
| Presentation |
| Session |
| Transport |
| Network |
| Data Link |
| Physical |

Figure 1.1 OSI reference model.

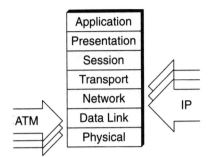

Figure 1.2   ATM and IP, with the OSI reference model.

ATM has its own reference model, which we look at in Chapter 8, "Asynchronous Transfer Mode." However, what is relevant here is that the OSI reference model between where ATM and IP operate overlaps. Chaos theorists often state that "the interesting stuff is in the boundaries," and there is plenty of interesting stuff in the boundaries where IP and ATM interoperate.

More differences between IP and ATM are laid out in Table 1.1. Also included in this table is a column for Ethernet that provides a baseline "normal" data link layer technology, something that has long worked quite nicely with IP. The reason these differences are laid out is to make clear that doing IP over ATM is not as simple as encapsulating an IP datagram inside an ATM frame.

Table 1.1   IP, ATM, and Ethernet

ATTRIBUTE	IP	ATM	ETHERNET
Switched or routed?	Routed	Switched	Both
Connection oriented or connectionless?	Connectionless	Connection-oriented	Connectionless
Quality of Service?	Yes, poorly understood	Yes, well understood	No
Native multicast/ broadcast support?	Yes	No	Yes
LAN or WAN?	Both	WAN	LAN
Desktop or backbone technology?	Both	Backbone	Both
Variable or fixed length units?	Variable	Fixed	Variable

What does this all mean? IP and Ethernet grew up together. To a certain extent, Ethernet and the 802.3 specifications created an open standard for the physical and data link layers upon which another open standard—IP—could flourish. On the other hand, ATM grew up in an entirely different standards environment—that of the telecommunications industry. It was designed initially as a mechanism for moving digitized voice communications across a network with the maximum performance, even during peak traffic periods. The telephone companies needed a mechanism by which they could transmit the bits that make up any number of different conversations over a single wire, optical fiber, or whatever network medium is being used. There could be no bottlenecks, so they had to break up each conversation into the smallest possible chunks. There had to be some way to guarantee service to prevent all the bits of one side of a conversation from being delivered all at once, so they decided to package all data into small, uniformly sized cells, none of which could hog a wire and keep other, more important traffic waiting. There also had to be a mechanism to differentiate between traffic that had to go through no matter what and traffic that would be nice to get through if there's enough room, so Quality of Service was added as a feature.

All ATM data is switched, rather than routed, meaning that two nodes communicating with each other must go through the process of signaling to determine how data is to be switched, that is, which switches will actually handle the bits of the interaction. Finally, as a connection-oriented network technology, ATM uses circuits to link nodes on the network. Every time one node wants to communicate with another node, it must create a circuit between itself and the destination node. Although this results in highly efficient results for node-to-node communication, it is suboptimal for broadcast or multicast transmissions. In order to deliver a broadcast message to all nodes on a logical IP subnet (LIS), an ATM node would have to, somehow, discover every other node connected to the same LIS, then go through the process of building up a separate circuit with each and every one of those nodes in order to deliver the broadcast message.

Broadcasts, though not encouraged for most applications, are quite central to some important IP protocols and applications. Multicast is an important mechanism for saving bandwidth, at least for the media that can support it (such as Ethernet), while supporting applications such as videoconferencing. The fact that ATM is not able to natively support multicast or broadcast tends to be a stumbling block for those who would like to take advantage of its speed and quality of service features to support multicast applications.

All this brings us back to the issue of ATM and IP standards.

ATM and IP Standards

ATM has its own set of standards, which we touch on briefly in Chapter 8. IP has *its* own standards, and we cover those in a very general way in the rest of the first part of this book, but you could fill several bookcases with volumes describing Internet standards. In the rest of this part of the book, we introduce the broad areas in which the intersection of ATM and IP have produced Internet standards-track specifications.

Internet specifications relevant for ATM fall into the following broad categories:

- How to do over ATM the IP things that would normally use broadcast and/or multicast
- How to encapsulate IP traffic inside ATM traffic
- How to support ATM quality of service within IP and IP applications
- How to route IP through ATM switched networks
- How to manage ATM networks using SNMP

The second part of this book examines each of these categories of Internet standards and proposed standards, as described in RFC documents.

CHAPTER 2

Internet Standards
and Internet Protocols

Many people consider Internet standards and Internet protocols almost magical. Although other standards may be more widely implemented, few are implemented in such a public way. Telecommunications protocols may affect more, but few standards are so interoperably implemented by so many different implementers. So what exactly makes a protocol an Internet standard? And what exactly is an Internet protocol?

As with so much else in life, these questions have two sets of answers. One set is simple, straightforward, and of limited practical usefulness. The other set, though more useful, is also far more involved. If you want the easy answers, you can find them in the next paragraph. If you want the useful answers, you'll have to read all the chapters in Part One of this book.

An Internet protocol is a set of rules that specifies interaction between networked entities over the Internet or other TCP/IP networks. A protocol becomes an Internet standard if it is listed as such in the Internet standards document known as STD-1. RFC 2500 defined current Internet standards as of its publication date: June 1999. STD-1 is published approximately once every 100 RFCs and lists the status of all current RFCs.

The complicated but useful answers require asking even more questions: What is an RFC? An STD? How are Internet protocols documented? What other kinds of documents are relevant to Internet protocols? How does a protocol differ from an application? What are the steps that must be taken to create an Internet standard? What, exactly, is a protocol? Do all RFCs describe Internet standards? Do all RFCs describe protocols? Is there a simple list of current Internet standards?

All these questions are answered in this chapter. Of course, the answers raise even more questions, which are answered in the coming chapters. Chapter 3, "Internet Standards Bodies," shows where Internet standards come from. Chapter 4, "The Internet Standards Process," examines how a protocol makes its way from being an idea to being an Internet standard. Chapter 5, "Getting the RFCs," identifies where to find documentation of current and future Internet standards. Chapter 6, "Reading the RFCs," tells you how to read and use RFCs and other related documents.

Internet Documents

The Request for Comments (RFC) represents the most important form Internet standards take and is the most often cited type of document when people speak of Internet standards. However, it is far from the only type of Internet standards-related document. RFCs represent an archive of all the wisdom of the Internet (as well as much else), from its very start in 1969.

Not all RFCs are readily available. Many early RFCs never made it into electronic format and have been lost over time. However, all the current RFCs with any relevance to the modern Internet are available online. Several different types of RFCs exist, including several special RFC series. In this section, we define the different categories of Internet documents.

RFCs

Any definition of the RFCs should start with that offered in RFC 2026, "The Internet Standards Process — Revision 3" (BCP 9):

```
Each distinct version of an Internet standards-related specification is
published as part of the "Request for Comments" (RFC) document series.
This archival series is the official publication channel for Internet
standards documents and other publications of the IESG, IAB, and
Internet community.  RFCs can be obtained from a number of Internet
hosts using anonymous FTP, gopher, World Wide Web, and other Internet
document-retrieval systems.
```

An RFC is simply a report, originally called a "Request for Comments" because researchers reported their own results, theories, and activities and solicited responses from other researchers through this mechanism. All Internet standards are published as RFCs, but not all RFCs document Internet standards. Publication of a document as an RFC may mean that it should be considered a standard, or it could simply mean that the RFC editor deemed it to be of interest or value to the Internet community.

Once published, an RFC is frozen in time. It can never be edited, updated, revised, or changed in any way. There is never any question of which is the most recent version of a particular RFC. RFC 2500, cited above, will never change, though the official protocol standards of the Internet are likely to change. Any changes will be documented in an RFC also titled "Internet Official Protocol Standards" (or something very much like that), but with a higher RFC number (probably 2600).

RFCs may be written by anyone: students, professors, researchers, employees of networking companies, employees of companies that use networking products, anyone. As long as the document has relevance for computer communications, is formatted appropriately, and submitted according to the rules (to be discussed in Chapter 4), it stands a chance of being published as an RFC.

RFCs may be reviewed prior to publication by the RFC editor, by Internet task forces, by one or more individual experts, or by anyone else the RFC editor deems appropriate, but RFCs are not technical refereed publications. When the author intends the document to specify an Internet standard, very specific steps must be taken to gain approval. These steps are detailed in Chapter 4.

STDs

The body of RFCs includes a few subsets of document series. Most important are the STDs (standards) documents. These are RFCs that document protocols that are considered to be Internet Standards with a capital S. The STD series clearly identifies the RFCs that document current Internet standards. An Internet standard protocol may have undergone several updates, revisions, or changes since it first was published as an RFC. The Internet STD series links specific protocols with static STD numbers. For example, the Simple Mail Transfer Protocol (SMTP) is an Internet standard and is described in STD-10. The most recent list of Internet standards identifies the STD-10 document as being RFC 821. Should an upgrade to SMTP be accepted as an Internet standard, STD-10 would no longer point to RFC 821, but rather to the new RFC that documents SMTP version 2 (be it called SMTP next generation or Complicated Mail Transfer Protocol, or whatever).

STDs point at the current standards and provide a point of reference for anyone looking for the most current version of Internet standards. STDs document standards rather than single protocols. A standard that comprises more than one protocol may have an STD that comprises more than one RFC. For example, STD-5 describes the standard for the Internet Protocol (IP) and it points to six different RFCs: RFC 791, RFC 950, RFC 951, RFC 919, RFC 792, and RFC 1112. These RFCs describe not only the Internet Protocol but also IP subnetting, IP broadcasting, IP broadcasting with subnets, the Internet Control Message Protocol (ICMP), and the Internet Group Multicast Protocol (IGMP), respectively.

When a specification reaches full standard status, it is assigned an STD number. When a full standard becomes obsolete, its STD number is not reused but is no longer included in the pantheon of Internet standards. For example, STD-4, "Gateway Requirements," was most recently documented in RFC 1009, "Requirements for Internet Gateways," and was phased out as a standard in RFC 1800 in 1995. In that version of the Internet Standards document, the protocol referenced by STD-4 became historic and STD-4 was retired. We come back to STD documents later in this chapter.

FYIs

In 1990, RFC 1150 "F.Y.I. on F.Y.I. Introduction to the F.Y.I. Notes" was published. The FYI documents described in RFC 1150 were intended to be a subset of the RFC document series:

```
The FYI series of notes is designed to provide Internet users with a
central repository of information about any topics which relate to
the Internet.  FYIs topics may range from historical memos on "Why it
was done this way" to answers to commonly asked operational
questions.
```

The FYI document, which is something like a cross between a primer and a FAQ, was intended to answer questions rather than to describe a specific protocol. All FYIs are RFCs, though not all RFCs are FYIs. FYIs refer to specific topics and point at RFCs, but when one RFC becomes obsolete or is replaced by another newer document, the FYI number may remain the same while it points to the newer document. FYI 1 points to RFC 1150. FYI 2 points to RFC 1470, "FYI on a Network Management

Tool Catalog: Tools for Monitoring and Debugging TCP/IP Internets and Interconnected Devices." FYI 5 points to RFC 1178, "1470—FYI on a Network Management Tool Catalog: Tools for Monitoring and Debugging TCP/IP Internets and Interconnected Devices."

BCPs

Members of another series of RFCs are called Best Current Practice (BCP) documents. RFC 1818, "Best Current Practices," describes the series as containing those documents that "best describe current practices for the Internet community." The rationale behind creating a new series of documents was that, at the time (November 1995), there were only two types of RFCs: standards track RFCs and all other RFCs.

The standards track RFCs are intended to document Internet standards, and documents are accepted into the standards track based on a very specific and rigorous process. The remaining RFCs consist of far less formal documents. These RFCs have no formal review or quality control process, which means that publication as a nonstandards track RFC affords relatively little standing for a document's content.

The Best Current Practices series provides the IETF with a mechanism to disseminate officially sanctioned technical information outside of protocol specifications. The sequence of review necessary for an RFC to be promoted to BCP status is similar to that required for an RFC to be promoted to an Internet standard, as we see in Chapter 4. While STDs describe protocols, BCPs describe other technical information that has been endorsed by the IETF.

BCPs can refer to meta-issues relating to the Internet, such as BCP 9: RFC 2026, "The Internet Standards Process—Revision 3." This document describes the process by which a protocol becomes a standard. BCPs may also refer to deployment or implementation issues, such as BCP 5: RFC 1918, "Address Allocation for Private Internets." This document provides guidelines for the efficient allocation of network addresses to avoid connectivity problems while at the same time conserving globally unique IP addresses, a depleted resource.

RTRs

RARE is the acronym for the Reseaux Associes pour la Recherche Europeenne (Association of European Research Networks). Its purpose is to create a high-quality computer communications infrastructure for Europe, using Open Systems Interconnection (OSI) protocols as well as

TCP/IP and related protocols. RARE Technical Reports (RTRs) are described in RFC 2151, "A Primer on Internet and TCP/IP Tools and Utilities" as being published as RFCs in order to promote cooperation between RARE and the Internet effort. For example, RTR 6 refers to RFC 1506, "A Tutorial on Gatewaying between X.400 and Internet Mail." RTRs often document issues related to interoperability between OSI and IP-related protocols.

Internet-Drafts

The documents that describe Internet standards as embodied in RFCs evolve over time and through many revisions before becoming RFCs, let alone Internet standards. Well before a standards-related specification is accepted as an RFC, it must start out as an Internet-Draft (I-D). As explained in RFC 2026, "The Internet Standards Process—Revision 3":

```
During the development of a specification, draft versions of the
document are made available for informal review and comment by
placing them in the IETF's "Internet-Drafts" directory, which is
replicated on a number of Internet hosts.  This makes an evolving
working document readily available to a wide audience, facilitating
the process of review and revision.
```

Unlike RFCs, which are intended to survive over time, unchanged and unchanging, I-Ds are meant to be temporary. They are working documents that are meant to be replaced once updated and forgotten when no longer useful. For example, all drafts must include an expiration date, and any published I-D that is not revised or accepted as an RFC after six months is "simply removed from the Internet-Drafts directory."

While RFCs are meant to be used as references, readers are warned *not* to use I-Ds as references. They have no formal status with the IETF. They are not archived, so references to specific versions of I-Ds can not be used. Readers are warned not to refer to I-Ds in other published materials other than as being "works in progress," and they are especially cautioned not claim compliance with specific I-Ds for their products.

We discuss I-Ds in more detail, particularly as they relate to the standards process, in Chapter 4.

Internet Standards

One might easily believe that an RFC either documents or does not document an Internet standard, but it isn't quite that simple. First, a handful of fundamental standards such as STD-1 actually describe the rest of the Internet standards. Other standards in this category include the Assigned Numbers document, which lists all values that have special meaning to Internet standards, and the host and router requirements specifications.

Standards themselves have two special characteristics: *state* and *status*. A standard's state refers to its maturity level: It might be a proposed standard, a draft standard, or an actual standard. The standard's status refers to its requirements level: Is the protocol required, recommended, or elective?

The term "Internet standard" refers specifically to a protocol that is either already accepted as a full Internet standard or that is on the Internet standard track. To discover what protocols and what RFCs are standards or on the standards track, you consult STD-1. The most recent version of STD-1—RFC 2500—lists not only all the current standards, but also the RFCs documenting draft standard and proposed standard protocols as well as informational and historic protocols.

STD-1 contains lists of current STDs along with the RFCs linked to each STD. STD-1 also lists all Internet protocols by their maturity level, as described below. This document is the key to all the Internet standards: If you want to know which protocols are standards and where those standards are documented, you simply locate the current document referenced by STD-1. All other STDs are listed here.

STD-2 is the Assigned Numbers document, most recently published as RFC 1700. STD-2 includes the most important numbers to the Internet. For example, this document lists the values of well-known ports, reserved multicast addresses, or virtually any values related to TCP/IP protocols. However, RFC 1700 was published in 1994 and is seriously out of date. The Internet Assigned Numbers Authority (IANA) has been publishing these values online, at www.iana.org/numbers.html. This will probably change as the IANA is replaced by the Internet Corporation for Assigned Names and Numbers (ICANN). Both IANA and ICANN, and the transition from one to the other, are discussed in Chapter 3.

Standards can be deprecated, meaning they are no longer considered standards. For example, between publication of RFC 2400 (September 1998) and publication of RFC 2500 (June 1999), STD-3, consisting of RFC 1122 and RFC 1123, was removed from the list of standards. These documents describe precisely what is expected from TCP/IP host implementations, and are now listed as Current Applicability Statements, meaning they describe the way Internet entities should behave. As mentioned earlier, STD-4 for gateway requirements is no longer listed. The term gateway is no longer considered appropriate, and the new standard refers to IP version 4 routers. RFC 1812 replaces the chain of obsolete specifications for IPv4 routers (starting with RFC 1009, "Standards Requirements for Internet Gateways"), but the related standard, STD-4, has long been absent from the list of current standards. RFC 2500 lists RFC 1812 as a proposed standard and does not show an STD document for IPv4 router requirements. That specification may eventually be promoted to full standard status, at which point it will receive a higher STD number—or (more likely) it will be designated a Current Applicability Statement.

States: Standards Maturity Levels

STD-1 defines a series of levels describing a standard's maturity. There are six levels defined, along with suggestions for where and when they should actually be implemented:

Standard Protocol. This is a protocol that has been established as an official standard protocol for the Internet by the IESG. Standard protocols define how things should be done. In other words, if you are going to do Internet routing, you must use the Internet standard routing protocols; if you are doing Internet email, you must the Internet standards for email. There should be no problems with interoperability if the protocol is implemented.

Draft Standard Protocol. A protocol that is under active consideration by the IESG to become a Standard Protocol is considered a draft standard. Draft standard protocols are likely to eventually be made standard. Wide implementation is desirable from the point of view of the standards bodies, as this provides a broader base for evaluating the protocol. Draft standards may be modified before being accepted as standards, and implementers must be prepared to accept and incorporate those changes.

Proposed Standard Protocol. A protocol being proposed for consideration as a standard sometime in the future by the IESG is called a Proposed Standard Protocol. These protocols need to be implemented and deployed in order to test them, but they are rarely accepted as standards without revisions.

Experimental Protocol. Protocols that are being used for experimentation or that are not related to operational services are considered experimental. If you are not in the experiment, you should not implement the experimental protocol, though the experiment will probably depend on all participants' implementing the protocol. Experimental protocols can later be admitted to the standards track, at which time their maturity level would be changed.

Informational Protocol. Protocols that have been developed outside the Internet development community—for example, those developed as proprietary protocols or those developed by other standards bodies—may be documented as informational protocols. These specifications can be published as RFCs for the convenience of the Internet community. Examples already cited include the NFS protocol developed by Sun and the CyberCash payment protocol.

Historical Protocol. Historical protocols are no longer relevant, either because they have been superseded by newer versions or by newer alternative protocols or because there was not sufficient interest to advance them through the standards process. These protocols are unlikely to ever become standards.

Standards maturity levels depend on context. A group of network-specific standard protocols have been defined for link layer protocols. Obviously, STD-42, "Internet Protocol on Ethernet Networks," will not be implemented on ATM networks. Likewise, there are relatively few full-fledged standard Internet protocols (see the section "What's Standard, What's Not"); however, quite a few draft and proposed standard protocols are widely implemented in popular commercial products. For example, the very popular Dynamic Host Configuration Protocol (DHCP) is a draft standard, as is the Multipurpose Internet Mail Extensions (MIME) protocol. Furthermore, the Internet Message Access Protocol (IMAP) and the Hypertext Transfer Protocol (HTTP) are both still proposed standards.

Status: Standards
Requirements Levels

Up until RFC 2400, STD-1 defined a protocol's status as its requirements level. These levels provided guidance as to whether the protocol should be implemented and included the following:

Required Protocol. Systems must implement required protocols.

Recommended Protocol. Systems should implement recommended protocols.

Elective Protocol. Systems may choose whether to implement elective protocols. However, if a system will be implementing a protocol of this type, it must implement exactly this protocol. Multiple elective protocols are often offered for general areas, such as routing or email.

Limited Use Protocol. Protocols may be limited due to the fact that they are experimental, provide limited functionality, or lack current relevance.

Not Recommended Protocol. Some protocols are considered not recommended for general use. They may have limited functionality, lack current relevance, be designed for special purposes, or be experimental.

To put the requirements levels into perspective, a system that implemented only the required protocols would probably be able to do little more than be visible on an IP network. Upper layer protocols such as the Transport Control Protocol (TCP) and the User Datagram Protocol (UDP) were recommended but not required. Such a minimal host would be able to do little more than respond to most network requests with error messages. Implementing all the recommended protocols would improve the situation to the point that such a host would be usable for most simple and typical network services. However, these distinctions have been removed as RFC 2500 defines RFCs simply by maturity level.

Internet Nonstandards

Although roughly 2,500 different RFCs have been published, most are not currently relevant to Internet standards. Some RFCs document protocols that are now obsolete, such as the Simple File Transfer Protocol (SFTP) documented in RFC 913. These protocols may once have been considered useful, but are no longer. These protocols are considered *historical protocols* because they are of interest only for historical purposes and are not intended to be implemented on current systems.

Some RFCs describe protocols that are proprietary and are considered to be *informational protocols*. These include documents such as RFC 1898, "CyberCash Credit Card Protocol Version 0.8," or RFC 1813, "NFS Version 3 Protocol Specification," which documents Sun Microsystems Inc.'s Network File System. These protocols are documented for different reasons, though usually to provide information to the community about the work being done by the owner of the protocol. For example, Sun's NFS protocol, while not an Internet standard, is certainly an important protocol and is documented so that others can write applications that are compatible with NFS.

Some RFCs are purely informational and do not document actual protocols. They may summarize meetings or describe approaches to specific networking problems taken by the author(s). Most informational RFCs are intended to provide important information or to raise important questions.

One subset of informational RFCs includes April Fool's documents, published on April 1 of each year and conforming strictly to the RFC format. For example, one of the best-known examples is RFC 1149, "A Standard for the Transmission of IP Datagrams on Avian Carriers," published April 1, 1990. The earliest example I found is RFC 748, "TEL-NET RANDOMLY-LOSE Option," published in 1978.

What's Standard, What's Not

The reader is directed to STD-1 for a complete survey of Internet standards, draft standards, proposed standards, and other protocols. Tables 2.1 and 2.2 list the current Internet standards and current network-specific standards, as they appear in RFC 2500.

Table 2.1   Internet Standards as Defined by RFC 2500 (STD-1)

PROTOCOL	NAME	RFC	STD
	Internet Official Protocol Standards	2500	1
	Assigned Numbers	1700	2
IP	Internet Protocol	791	5
	as amended by:--------		
	IP Subnet Extension	950	5
	IP Broadcast Datagrams	919	5
	IP Broadcast Datagrams with Subnets	922	5
ICMP	Internet Control Message Protocol	792	5
IGMP	Internet Group Multicast Protocol	1112	5

Continues

Table 2.1   Internet Standards as Defined by RFC 2500 (STD-1)   *(Continued)*

PROTOCOL	NAME	RFC	STD
UDP	User Datagram Protocol	768	6
TCP	Transmission Control Protocol	793	7
TELNET	Telnet Protocol	854,855	8
FTP	File Transfer Protocol	959	9
SMTP	Simple Mail Transfer Protocol	821	10
SMTP-SIZE	SMTP Service Ext for Message Size	1870	10
SMTP-EXT	SMTP Service Extensions	1869	10
MAIL	Format of Electronic Mail Messages	822	11
NTPV2	Network Time Protocol (Version 2)	1119	12
DOMAIN	Domain Name System	1034,1035	13
DNS-MX	Mail Routing and the Domain System	974	14
SNMP	Simple Network Management Protocol	1157	15
SMI	Structure of Management Information	1155	16
Concise-MIB	Concise MIB Definitions	1212	16
MIB-II	Management Information Base-II	1213	17
NETBIOS	NetBIOS Service Protocols	1001,1002	19
ECHO	Echo Protocol	862	20
DISCARD	Discard Protocol	863	21
CHARGEN	Character Generator Protocol	864	22
QUOTE	Quote of the Day Protocol	865	23
USERS	Active Users Protocol	866	24
DAYTIME	Daytime Protocol	867	25
TIME	Time Server Protocol	868	26
TOPT-BIN	Binary Transmission	856	27
TOPT-ECHO	Echo	857	28
TOPT-SUPP	Suppress Go Ahead	858	29
TOPT-STAT	Status	859	30
TOPT-TIM	Timing Mark	860	31
TOPT-EXTOP	Extended-Options-List	861	32

Table 2.1 *(Continued)*

PROTOCOL	NAME	RFC	STD
TFTP	Trivial File Transfer Protocol	1350	33
TP-TCP	ISO Transport Service on top of the TCP	1006	35
ETHER-MIB	Ethernet MIB	1643	50
PPP	Point-to-Point Protocol (PPP)	1661	51
PPP-HDLC	PPP in HDLC Framing	1662	51
IP-SMDS	IP Datagrams over the SMDS Service	1209	52
POP3	Post Office Protocol, Version 3	1939	53
OSPF2	Open Shortest Path First Routing V2	2328	54
IP-FR	Multiprotocol over Frame Relay	2427	55
RIP2	RIP Version 2-Carrying Additional Info.	2453	56
RIP2-APP	RIP Version 2 Protocol App. Statement	1722	57
SMIv2	Structure of Management Information v2	2578	58
CONV-MIB	Textual Conventions for SNMPv2	2579	58
CONF-MIB	Conformance Statements for SNMPv2	2580	58

Table 2.2 Network-specific Draft, Proposed, and Standard Protocols, as Defined by RFC 2500 (STD-1)

PROTOCOL	NAME	STATUS	RFC	STD
IP-ATM	Classical IP and ARP over ATM	Prop	2225	
ATM-ENCAP	Multiprotocol Encapsulation over ATM	Prop	1483	
IP-TR-MC	IP Multicast over Token-Ring LANs	Prop	1469	
IP-FDDI	Transmission of IP and ARP over FDDI Net	Std	1390	36
IP-X.25	X.25 and ISDN in the Packet Mode	Draft	1356	
ARP	Address Resolution Protocol	Std	826	37
RARP	A Reverse Address Resolution Protocol	Std	903	38
IP-ARPA	Internet Protocol on ARPANET	Std	BBN1822	39
IP-WB	Internet Protocol on Wideband Network	Std	907	40
IP-E	Internet Protocol on Ethernet Networks	Std	894	41
IP-EE	Internet Protocol on Exp. Ethernet Nets	Std	895	42

Continues

Table 2.2   Network-specific Draft, Proposed, and Standard Protocols, as Defined by RFC 2500 (STD-1) *(Continued)*

PROTOCOL	NAME	STATUS	RFC	STD
IP-IEEE	Internet Protocol on IEEE 802	Std	1042	43
IP-DC	Internet Protocol on DC Networks	Std	891	44
IP-HC	Internet Protocol on Hyperchannel	Std	1044	45
IP-ARC	Transmitting IP Traffic over ARCNET Nets	Std	1201	46
IP-SLIP	Transmission of IP over Serial Lines	Std	1055	47
IP-NETBIOS	Transmission of IP over NETBIOS	Std	1088	48
IP-IPX	Transmission of 802.2 over IPX Networks	Std	1132	49
IP-HIPPI	IP over HIPPI	Draft	2067	

Reading List

Table 2.3 contains some RFCs that elaborate on the information presented in this chapter.

For the most current assigned numbers, check out the Current Assigned Numbers Web site at www.iana.org/numbers.html.

Another good resource is the Internet Mail Consortium's (IMC) IETF Novice's Guide, at: www.imc.org/novice-ietf.html.

Table 2.3   Relevant RFCs

RFC	TITLE	DESCRIPTION
RFC 2500	Internet Official Protocol Standards	This is the current incarnation of Internet STD-1 and includes complete information about Internet standards current when the RFC was published.
RFC 1700	Assigned Numbers	This is the most recent publication of the assigned numbers document. It documents assigned numbers that were current when the RFC was published.
RFC 1150	F.Y.I. on F.Y.I.—Introduction to the F.Y.I. Notes	This RFC explains what the F.Y.I. series of documents is all about.
RFC 1818	Best Current Practices	This RFC explains the best current practices series.
RFC 2026	The Internet Standards Process—Revision 3	This RFC explains how specifications become Internet standards. We return to cover the material in this RFC in depth in Chapter 4.

Internet Standards Bodies

A regular alphabet-soup of standards bodies guide, cajole, steer, and engineer standards into existence. Learning what each group does, how each group relates to the other groups, and how the groups are involved in the standards development process will help you to understand how Internet standards work. With this understanding you will be better equipped to track the standards process and make appropriate decisions about how to use those standards in your organization and products.

Some Internet standards bodies have been documented in RFCs; others make their charters available on the Internet through their Web sites. Still other standards bodies are not, strictly speaking, part of the Internet standards process, but their work affects Internet standards in some way or other. This chapter introduces the most important players in the standards process, starting with Internet groups and followed by introductions to other important standards groups. The end of the chapter has references to relevant RFCs as well as URLs pointing to organizational Web sites.

The organizations that are involved in the Internet standards process are highly interrelated and interdependent. It is almost impossible to talk about one of them without making reference to one or more of the others. Figure 3.1 shows a simplified organizational chart that displays the relationships among the bodies that are important to the creation of Internet standards. Each of these bodies is explained in this chapter.

The IAB

The Internet Architecture Board (IAB), which was originally called the Internet Activities Board when it was first set up in 1983, did not begin publishing its activities until 1990, so much of its origins are misted by time and memory. IAB chair Brian Carpenter wrote an overview of the IAB in 1996, called "What Does the IAB Do, Anyway?" (available online at www.iab.org/connexions.html). RFC 1160, published in 1990, provides an early history and description of the IAB. The IAB charter is documented in RFC 1601. These documents form the basis of this section, which details the IAB and what it does.

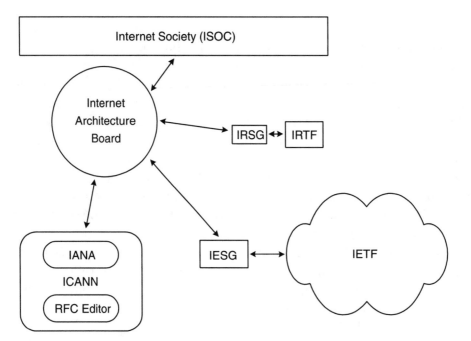

Figure 3.1   A simple organizational chart showing the links among the primary bodies involved in the development of Internet standards.

IAB History

According to RFC 1160, Internet research during the 1970s slowly grew to the point where it became necessary to form a committee that could guide development of the protocol suite. This committee was called the Internet Configuration Control Board (ICCB). In January 1983, the Defense Communications Agency declared the TCP/IP protocol suite to be the standard for the Advanced Research Projects Agency network, also known as the ARPANET. The Defense Communications Agency was the organization within the U.S. government responsible for operation of the ARPANET, which later evolved into the Internet. Later in 1983, DARPA reorganized the ICCB and renamed it the Internet Activities Board.

As of 1990, the IAB had only two important task forces—the Internet Engineering Task Force (IETF) and the Internet Research Task Force (IRTF)—both of which were established in 1986. Each task force is led by a chairman and guided by a steering group: the Internet Engineering Steering Group (IESG) for the IETF, and the Internet Research Steering Group (IRSG) for the IRTF. Most of the work of the task forces is carried out by working groups (WGs) set up for specific programs or topics.

In 1992, the IAB was reconstituted as a component of the Internet Society (ISOC), and its name was changed from the Internet Activities Board to the Internet Architecture Board. We discuss the Internet Society and the other organizational components mentioned in the charter, including the IETF, the IESG, the IRTF, and the IRSG, at greater length later in this chapter.

IAB Charter

The charter, published as RFC 1601, is a good place to start to understand what the IAB is and what function it fulfills. We begin by outlining the IAB's functions. According to RFC 1601, the IAB's responsibilities are:

1. Selection of Internet Engineering Steering Group (IESG) members. The charter calls for a fair degree of unanimity, requiring at least eight votes in favor of a successful nominee and no more than one vote against the nominee.

2. Provide architectural oversight for Internet protocols and procedures. An important function of the IAB is long-range planning. The charter calls for the IAB to track the important long-term issues relevant to the Internet and to make sure that the groups that should address the issues are made aware of those issues. The

IAB is responsible for organizing the Internet Research Task Force (IRTF) as part of its architectural oversight function.

3. Provide oversight to the Internet standards process as well as provide an appeals board for complaints about that process. The IAB, with the participation of the IESG, defines how that process is to unfold and also documents that process.

4. Manage and publish the RFC document series and administer the Internet assigned numbers. It is up to the IAB to select an RFC editor (Jonathan B. Postel, Ph.D., was RFC editor until his untimely passing in October 1998). The RFC editor is responsible for the editorial management and publication of the RFC series. According to its charter, the IAB is also responsible for designating an Internet Assigned Numbers Authority (IANA) to administer the assignment of Internet protocol numbers. Jon Postel was also responsible as the IANA, and this function will pass to the ICANN.

5. Act on behalf of the Internet Society as liaison with other organizations that are concerned with global Internet standards, technologies, and organizational issues. Some of the entities the IAB liaises with include the U.S. Federal Networking Council (FNC); various organs of the European Commission (EC); the Coordinating Committee for Intercontinental Research Networking (CCIRN); standards bodies such as the International Organization for Standardization (ISO), the International Electrotechnical Commission (IEC), and the International Telecommunication Union (ITU); and other professional societies such as the Institute of Electrical and Electronic Engineers (IEEE) and the Association for Computing Machinery (ACM).

6. Provide advice to the Internet Society, guiding the trustees and offices of the Internet Society on technologies, architecture, procedures, and, where appropriate, policy matters that relate to the Internet and related technologies. Where necessary, the IAB can call together expert panels, hold hearings, or use other methods to investigate questions or issues raised by the Internet Society.

The IAB is made up of 13 voting members, including the IETF chair and 12 full members. The IETF chair is also the IESG chair and gets a vote on all IAB actions with one exception: the approval of IESG members. Full IAB members serve for two years and are permitted to serve for any number of terms. Although IAB members may have day jobs, they must act as individuals on the board and not as representatives of any employer.

The IETF, through a nominating committee, nominates IAB members. The Internet Society Board of Trustees votes on the nominees for IAB membership. The IAB chair is voted on by the current twelve sitting IAB members. The charter states that normally six new full members are nominated each year. The charter also specifies who is eligible for the nomination committee.

How the IAB Works

The IAB usually meets about once a month through a telephone conference, according to Brian Carpenter. These meetings usually run about two hours each and are scheduled to allow members from all parts of the world to participate, though not always without some inconvenient scheduling. Physical meetings occur three times a year at IETF meetings, at which the IAB also holds an open meeting that allows any IETF member to raise issues directly with the IAB.

As we see later when we discuss the actual standards process, the IAB itself does not drive the technical work so much as oversee and guide it. This means that during IAB meetings, action is not necessarily taken on specific standards or protocols. More often, apart from the usual administrivia of reviewing action lists, the IAB attempts to strategize in depth on one or two important issues and come up with some result that can be passed along to the relevant entities: the IESG, IETF working groups, or the public, though an RFC.

Carpenter gives some examples of issues that were raised during IAB meetings held during the second half of 1995, including:

- The future of Internet addressing
- Architectural principles of the Internet
- Future goals and directions for the IETF
- Management of top-level domains in the Domain Name System
- Registration of MIME types
- International character sets
- Charging for addresses
- Tools needed for renumbering

Rather than attempting to come up with solutions to the issues that are raised, the IAB's aim is either to get the IESG to take action or to stimulate the IETF community to address the issues. When the IAB publishes RFCs or Internet-Drafts, they are in the form of statements or viewpoints rather than actual proposals for new or modified standards.

The IAB can also initiate workshops or panels that operate outside the standards process but that are intended to incubate ideas in specific areas. Carpenter cites workshops held on security, which is documented in RFC 1636, and on information infrastructure, which is documented in RFC 1862. The IAB may also initiate the formation of research groups under the aegis of the IRTF. However, the research groups are not intended to generate standards-track proposals, unlike the workshops or panels research groups, which are intended to persist over time.

According to Carpenter, in between meetings, IAB members keep track of relevant IETF and IESG activities through email lists and by commenting on draft charters of new working groups, reviewing documents that are in the last stages of getting approval, and generally helping out when difficulties arise with working groups.

Carpenter makes clear also what the IAB is not: The IETF is the standards body, the IAB is drawn from the IETF. The IAB is mostly an advisory board and has minimal input to policy issues for the Internet. The IAB might decide it is important that work be done on some kind of standard, but it can not specify where and whether that standard must be applied. In practice, though, the boundaries between the IETF, the IESG, and the IAB are blurred, and those borders are not strictly patrolled but rather used as guidelines for action.

The Internet Society

The Internet Society, also known as ISOC, was announced in 1991 and born as an organization in January 1992. It is "the international organization for global cooperation and coordination for the Internet and its internetworking technologies and applications," according to the FAQ page on the ISOC Web site. It is a not-for-profit organization with tax-deductible status based in Reston, Virginia.

Though it boasts a membership of individuals and organizations representing all segments of the global Internet community, as of early 1999 it claimed only about 7,000 members worldwide. ISOC's mission statement is "To assure the beneficial, open evolution of the global

Internet and its related internetworking technologies through leadership in standards, issues, and education." The Internet Society mission continues:

> Since 1992, the Internet Society has served as the international organization for global coordination and cooperation on the Internet, promoting and maintaining a broad spectrum of activities focused on the Internet's development, availability, and associated technologies.

The Internet Society acts not only as a global clearinghouse for Internet information and education but also as a facilitator and coordinator of Internet-related initiatives around the world. Through its annual International Networking (INET) conference and other sponsored events, developing-country training workshops, tutorials, statistical and market research, publications, public policy and trade activities, regional and local chapters, standardization activities, committees, and an international secretariat, the Internet Society serves the needs of the growing global Internet community. From commerce to education to social issues, its goal is to enhance the availability and utility of the Internet on the widest possible scale.

In terms of the number of individuals and organizations affected, the Internet Society's most important activities are those related to Internet standards. The Internet Society was founded, in part, to provide an ongoing source of organizational and financial support for the IETF and other related bodies. By the early 1990s, it was apparent that the involvement of the U.S. government as the primary supporter of Internet activities could not be sustained. To grow, the Internet had to move from being a research and academic tool to being a medium for commercial development, and it was clear that the U.S. government would eventually stop funding the Internet. In addition to funding the IAB, IETF, and other related groups, the Internet Society's board of directors, consisting of 15 Internet deities, is responsible for approving IAB members that have been nominated by the IETF nominating committee. Chapter 4, "The Internet Standards Process," outlines how the Internet Society participates in the Internet standards process.

The IETF and IESG

It may seem that the IETF would be a formal organization with membership lists, formal structure, and activities. However, this is not the case. As is explained in RFC 1718, "The Tao of the IETF," the IETF is open to anyone who shows up. According to RFC 1718, the "Internet Engineering Task Force is a loosely self-organized group of people who make technical and other contributions to the engineering and evolution of the Internet and its technologies." You can participate at any of the three yearly meetings in person, or you can participate through IETF working groups and their mailing lists.

The individuals who participate in the IETF include network designers, operators, vendors, researchers, and anyone else with an interest in the development of the Internet and its protocols and architecture. Within the IETF, most of the work is accomplished in working groups, which are categorized into different areas. We return to how working groups actually work in Chapter 4, but these are the IETF areas:

Applications Area includes working groups that address applications—in other words, anything that provides some benefit to end users—and excludes anything related to security, networks, transport protocols, or administration and management. Examples of working groups in this area include the Hypertext Transfer Protocol (HTTP), calendaring and scheduling, Internet fax, and others.

General Area currently includes only two working groups, the Policy Framework working group and the Process for Organization of Internet Standards working group. These groups address general areas of interest to the IETF.

Internet Area includes groups working on issues related directly to the Internet Protocol (IP), including groups working on implementing IP over different data link layer protocols as well as IPng (IP, next generation, now known as IPv6) and others.

Operations and Management Area working groups address issues related to the way things work on the Internet. Working groups in this area include a benchmarking group, a group working on year 2000 issues, groups working on network management protocols, and others.

Routing Area working groups focus on issues related to routing in the Internet. Working groups address multicast routing issues, quality of service routing issues, and others.

Security Area working groups focus on providing security to the protocols that other IETF groups are working on. Important working groups in this area include those addressing the IP security architecture (IPsec), groups working on various aspects of authentication, groups working on encryption issues, groups working on development of secure applications, and others.

Transport Area working groups focus on issues related to transport protocols as well as related protocols. For example, working groups include differentiated services, multicast address allocation, TCP implementation, and others.

User Services Area working groups focus on issues related to improving the quality of information available to Internet users and to developing programs that may be helpful to users. The three current working groups in this area are the Responsible Use of the Network group, the Site Security Handbook group, and the User Services group.

Most of these areas have a dozen or so working groups, and altogether there are well over 100 IETF working groups. Each IETF area has one or two area directors, who oversee and coordinate the activities of the workgroups in their areas. Each working group has one or two chairs, as well as an area advisor (usually one of the area directors).

Although the IETF can be a diffuse and somewhat nebulous organization, the Internet Engineering Steering Group is more explicitly and narrowly defined. The IETF area directors plus the IETF chair make up the IESG. Although all Internet protocol development work is done at the working group level, once the working groups are finished, it is the IESG that must approve the standard protocol specifications (or other documents) for publication as RFCs.

The Internet Research Task Force and Internet Research Steering Group

The Internet Research Task Force (IRTF) and the Internet Research Steering Group (IRSG) are not nearly as well known as the IETF and IESG. This is, in part, because the results of the IRTF research groups tend to be used as the basis for engineering work done by the IETF. Thus, while the results of the work done by IETF working groups may be enshrined as Internet standards, the results of the work done by IRTF research groups more often are used as one of many sources for new work by the IETF working groups.

The IRTF mission, stated on the IRTF Web page (www.irtf.org), is "To promote research of importance to the evolution of the future Internet by creating focused, long-term and small research groups working on topics related to Internet protocols, applications, architecture and technology." The activities of the IRTF research groups are thus more forward-looking than those of the IETF working groups: Their results may be published in peer-reviewed academic journals as well as in informational RFCs. An important difference between the IRTF research groups and IETF working groups is that membership in research groups is not necessarily open to all interested parties.

IRTF research groups currently include the following:

The End-to-End research group is concerned with issues related to end-to-end services and protocols, with particular attention to performance, traffic control, scheduling, protocol framing, efficient protocol implementations, high-performance host interfaces, and others.

The Information Infrastructure Architecture research group is concerned with developing an interoperable framework for the Internet's information architecture. Membership in this group is by invitation only.

The Internet Resource Discovery research group's mission is to develop a model by which resources can be described on the Internet. This includes the design of entities that can act on behalf of electronic resources for the purposes of indexing, querying, and retrieving information; building mechanisms that can create, maintain, and use data for those entities; and setting requirements for systems that use these entities. Membership in this group is by invitation only.

The Routing research group works on routing issues that have relevance to the Internet but that are not yet mature enough to be incorporated into work being done by IETF routing working groups. Some of the topics set forth in this group's charter include work on quality of service (QoS) routing, scalable multicast routing, routing protocol stability, and extremely dynamic routing. According to the charter, this group has a limited core membership but occasionally holds open meetings to solicit input from the rest of the community.

The Services Management research group works on issues related to the concept of "service management." Basing their work on the assumption that network management and system management are converging toward a single function, called service management, this group is investigating how best to go about creating new architectures and protocols that would allow a system/network manager to manage all different types of connected devices—from PDAs to mainframes—with the same conceptual framework and the same tool or tools. Membership in this group is by invitation only.

The Reliable Multicast research group, presumably, will be concerned with issues related to building a framework for doing multicasting reliably. However, the group's charter has not yet been published.

The Internet Research Steering Group (IRSG) membership is, like the IESG, limited to the chairs of all the research groups as well as the IRTF chair. Other prominent members of the community may be invited to serve as members of the IRSG.

Although some of these research groups maintain mailing lists or Web sites, some appear to be moribund. The address given for subscribing to the Internet Resource Discovery group mailing list is no longer valid, and other groups' mailing lists are sparsely attended. In fact, the Privacy and Security group is included on the IRTF Web site, but the group was disbanded in early 1998 because much of the group's work was done. The charter describes work that eventually resulted in the IP Security Architecture, a set of standards that have already been published in two versions as RFCs.

Internet Assigned Numbers Authority and Internet Corporation for Assigned Names and Numbers

As far as this book is concerned, the most important function of the Internet Assigned Numbers Authority (IANA) is to administer and publish numbers that are related to Internet standards. For example, if you want to know what different values in the IP header's protocol field represent, you would consult the IANA. Any arbitrary values related to Internet protocols and parameters must be assigned through the mediation of the IANA. You may not simply choose some value and then publish it as a standard. This goes for protocol parameters as well as well-known port numbers for transport layer protocols and any other number related to a protocol or an Internet standard.

However, as mentioned in Chapter 2, "Internet Standards and Internet Protocols" the IANA is in the process of being replaced by the Internet Corporation for Assigned Names and Numbers (ICANN). The need for a transition was apparent by 1996, when discussions and proposals began over how best to convert the U.S. government-funded IANA into an organization that could satisfactorily serve a global commercial Internet. Not only is the IANA responsible for protocol parameters, but it is also tasked with administering the assignment of globally unique Internet network addresses and domain names.

Internet addresses and domain names have a commercial component, as they are viewed as limited resources. There are only seven root-level three-letter domains (.gov, .mil, .edu, .int, .net, .org, and .com). Only three of these are generally available to businesses and organizations (.net, .org, and .com). There are issues relating to the way protected corporate trade names are allowed to be registered, as well as concern that additional root-level domains should be added. As for Internet network addresses, experts have been predicting since the late 1980s that the current version of IP (IPv4) does not provide a sufficiently large address space to support the continued growth of the Internet for many more years. These numbers are allocated through regional registries and are becoming more and more scarce.

After considerable debate and much revising, the ICANN proposal was accepted in late 1998—just a month and a half after Postel's death. The U.S. government acknowledged in a memorandum of understanding, dated November 25, 1998, that ICANN would be set up as a private, nonprofit corporation to administer policy for the Internet Name and Address System. The most visible and politically sensitive issues were the way addresses and domains are assigned, but the administration of protocol parameters will also be transferred to the ICANN because it was also part of the IANA's original charter.

Exactly how that function will be performed is yet to be seen. ICANN may simply continue to publish the assigned numbers online in the same way the IANA has been. In fact, by summer of 1999, ICANN's future, scope, form, and function were still unclear. ICANN funding was far from certain, and its precise duties were still undefined as were the ways in which it would interact with the Internet Society and the IETF.

More details are available at the IANA and ICANN Web sites for updates or subscribe to the ICANN-announce mailing list by sending a message to:

```
majordomo@icann.org
```

The message should have no subject line and the following command as the message body:

```
subscribe icann-announce
```

Other Relevant Bodies

Many more standards relate to networking and the Internet than those specified by the bodies described so far. Four of the most important other standards bodies are the World Wide Web Consortium (W3C), the International Telecommunication Union (ITU), the Institute of Electrical and Electronics Engineers (IEEE), and the National Institute of Standards and Technology. These bodies are profiled briefly below.

W3C

The World Wide Web Consortium (W3C) is the newest of the related standards bodies, founded in 1994 to promote the World Wide Web and help it achieve its full potential through the development of common and interoperable protocols. However, to the extent that work on important Internet protocols like Hypertext Transfer Protocol (HTTP) and the Universal Resource Identifier (URI) is done in partnership with the IETF, the W3C is most closely related to Internet standards.

Unlike the IETF, which is a wide-open organization, the W3C is an industry consortium. Individuals may join, but they must pay the full annual fee of $5,000, which is charged to affiliate organizational members (full members pay $50,000 each year). Unlike the IETF, when members suggest programs within the W3C, they must also back up the program proposal with funding for the work.

Operating out of the Laboratory for Computer Science at MIT, the W3C's members often are current or former contributors to Internet standards through the IETF. The two organizations share the goal of building interoperable protocols that foster connectivity without regard to nationality, corporate affiliation, or any other restrictive notions.

The W3C is organized into four different domains: User Interface, Technology & Society, Architecture, and the Web Accessibility Initiative. Each domain is responsible for different activity areas, resulting in an organization similar to that of the IETF areas and working groups.

The User Interface domain activity areas address issues that include data representations through the Hypertext Markup Language (HTML), stylesheets, fonts, internationalization, and others.

The Technology & Society domain activity areas address issues that include legal and social implications of the web, in particular electronic commerce, privacy concerns, digital signatures, and others.

The Architecture domain activity areas concern themselves with issues relating to the way the Web operates. Activity areas are devoted to issues like HTTP, structured document interchange using the Extensible Markup Language (XML), Synchronized Multimedia (SMIL), and others.

The Web Accessibility Initiative domain is chartered to pursue a high degree of usability for people with disabilities, through improved technology, guidelines, tools, education, and research.

As an industry consortium whose members are almost exclusively organizations, the W3C standards process is less open than that of the IETF, though interested readers will find the process document at www.w3.org/Consortium/Process/. W3C standards start out as Working Drafts and proceed to the status of Proposed Recommendations and finally Recommendations after passing through all review stages described in the process document. There are two other types of W3C documents, called Notes and Submissions. A Note is a document that the W3C publishes because it may be of interest to the community. Publication as a Note does not imply that the W3C endorses the document. W3C Submissions permit members to publish ideas or technologies for the consortium's consideration. Although the Notes are chosen by the W3C for publication, Submissions that are submitted with all support materials in order will be published. However, Submissions have no official status as W3C standards.

Because the IETF and the W3C share some of the same concerns, a high degree of cross-pollination goes on between the two organizations. Anyone interested in protocols related to the World Wide Web will find standards and protocols through both organizations. Where overlap occurs, the two organizations cooperate in the interests of interoperability.

IEEE

The Institute of Electrical and Electronics Engineers (IEEE) is an international professional organization for engineers. Founded in 1884, the IEEE standards groups work on specifications for all types of engineering pursuits including networking. In particular, IEEE standards are used to define the way data is transmitted across network media like ethernet. Important standards include the IEEE 802 LAN/MAN standards relating to ethernet transmissions, the IEEE P1394.1 high-performance serial bus bridge standards, and the IEEE P1363 standards for public-key cryptography.

ITU

With roots going back to the 1865 founding of the International Telegraph Union, the International Telecommunication Union (ITU) is one of the oldest standards bodies around. In 1947, it became an agency of the United Nations and is based in Geneva, Switzerland. Initially, it was set up to foster international standards for telegraphy, technical standards as well as standards for operations, tariffs, and telecommunications accounting practices. The ITU has evolved over the years to accommodate changes in the telecommunications industries it serves. Its activities include work on all sorts of data transmission media, including satellite, radio, and more traditional cabled transmission.

As telecommunications organizations increasingly rely on IP networks to carry voice as well as data, the ITU will expand its Internet-related activities. RFC 2436 addresses issues of interaction between the ITU and the IETF. The ITU currently has several study groups working on IP-related issues, including multimedia services and systems, telecommunication management networks and network maintenance, and signaling requirements and protocols for network media like ISDN. Other standards are developed through ITU, in particular the X.400 standards relating to message handling and the X.500 standards relating to directory services.

NIST

The National Institute of Standards and Technology (NIST) is an agency of the U.S. Department of Commerce's Technology Administration whose mission is to promote U.S. economic growth by working with industry to develop and apply technology, measurements, and standards. NIST is active in a number of important areas relating to the Internet, including standards for encryption such as the Data Encryption Standard (DES) and selection of a replacement for DES, known as the Advanced Encryption Standard (AES). NIST is also active in working on new protocols for broadband data transmission across high-speed networks including ATM, as well as research on technologies to support the next-generation Internet.

Reading List

RFC 2028, "The Organizations Involved in the IETF Standards Process," is a good place to start if you're interested in reading more. Table 3.1 includes Web sites for the organizations described in RFC 2028 as well as many others of relevance to the Internet standards process.

Table 3.1   Organizations Involved in the Internet Standards Process

ORGANIZATION	URL
The Internet Society (ISOC)	www.isoc.org
The Internet Corporation for Assigned Names and Numbers (ICANN)	www.icann.org
The Internet Assigned Numbers Authority (IANA)	www.iana.org/index2.html
The IANA Protocol Numbers and Assignment Services page	www.iana.org/numbers.html
The Internet Engineering Task Force (IETF)	www.ietf.org
The Internet Research Task Force (IRTF)	www.irtf.org
The Internet Engineering Steering Group (IESG)	www.ietf.org/iesg.html
The Internet Architecture Board (IAB)	www.iab.org/iab/
The World Wide Web Consortium (W3C)	www.w3c.org/
The International Telecommunication Union (ITU)	www.itu.int/
The Institute of Electrical and Electronics Engineers (IEEE)	www.ieee.org/
The IEEE Standards site	http://standards.ieee.org/

The Internet Standards Process

We've discussed what an Internet standard is in Chapter 2, "Internet Standards and Internet Protocols," and what organizations participate in the creation of Internet standards in Chapter 3, "Internet Standards Bodies." In this chapter, we look at the process by which a protocol becomes an Internet standard protocol. Working from two RFCs that describe the standards process and provide guidelines for IETF working groups, we introduce the activities necessary to create an Internet standard. In the last part of this chapter, we examine the instructions to RFC authors to better understand how those documents are structured and what information those documents contain.

The Standards Process

The abstract of RFC 2026, "The Internet Standards Process—Revision 3," reads:

```
This memo documents the process used by the Internet community for
the standardization of protocols and procedures.  It defines the
stages in the standardization process, the requirements for moving a
```

```
document between stages and the types of documents used during this
process.  It also addresses the intellectual property rights and
copyright issues associated with the standards process.
```

This RFC is currently defined as BCP-9, documenting the best current practices for defining Internet standards. The actual procedures required to turn a protocol into a standard are defined here. The document notes that specifications developed through the actions of the IAB and IETF are usually revised before becoming standards. However, specifications that have been defined by outside bodies may go through the same approval process that home-grown standards do, but the outside standards are not revised. In these cases, the Internet standards process is used to affirm it as a standard and to determine how it should be applied to the Internet, rather than to modify the specification being taken.

RFC 2026 defines the Internet standard, pointing out that the specification must be stable and well understood and must be competent technically. It should also have been implemented by more than one independent group, and all those implementations should be interoperable. There should be "substantial operational experience" with the standard, and the standard should enjoy "significant public support." Furthermore, it should be "recognizably useful in some or all parts of the Internet."

In a perfect world, the Internet standard process would be straightforward: Someone proposes a new protocol or process, people work on it over time, the Internet community provides feedback as the standard is gradually improved until the community determines that the specification is stable, competent, interoperable, supported, and is "recognizably useful." However, in practice, the difference between theory and practice is far greater than the difference between theory and practice, in theory. Defining Internet standards can be a messy process.

Standards Actions

As RFC 2026 makes clear, Internet *standards actions* must all be approved by the IESG, and standards actions include anything that modifies the state of the specification as it relates to the standards process. Anything that changes the state of a specification is a standards action. Actions occur when a specification enters the standards track, when it changes its maturity level within the standards track, or when it is removed from the standards track. None of those things can happen unless the IESG approves it.

The IESG follows guidelines devised to identify specifications that are ripe for a standard action, but the documented criteria are not hard-and-fast rules but rather guidelines. These guidelines will be discussed later. The IESG, as a group, uses its own judgment when deciding on standards actions. It has the power to deny an action to a specification that otherwise might appear to fulfill all requirements or to approve an action for a specification that might appear to fall short in one or more areas. If any parties believe that a standard action was granted or denied in error, they can resort to the dispute resolution procedures discussed later in this section.

The first step in the standards process is the entity sponsoring the specification publishing it as an Internet-Draft (I-D). Normally, this entity is the IETF working group, but it may also be an individual or some other organization. I-Ds produced by individuals or groups not directly connected to an IETF working group can be published as standards-track RFCs and are frequently published as informational RFCs as well. I-Ds are subject to modification based on community review, are transient documents, and are not intended to be referenced in the same way that RFCs are. I-Ds expire if they have not been modified for six months, though the timer starts again when a new version is published. An I-D published on January 1, 2001 would expire after June 30, 2001 if it was not revised; if a revision is published on June 1, 2001, then it is due to expire after November 30, 2001. If a revision is published January 15, 2001, then that I-D expires after July 15, 2001.

However, the whole point of publishing an I-D is to have it accepted to the Standards Track rather than to have it persist as an I-D. This is the first standards action that must occur in the standards process for any specification. No action can occur until the I-D has been available online for at least two weeks. This time is to be used for community review, allowing members of the IETF and the rest of the world to read the draft and make comments on it.

Although the IESG can't take any action until at least two weeks after the I-D is published, nothing happens unless the IETF working group makes a recommendation to its area director. It can take quite some time and several revisions before the working group makes that recommendation. Normally, one or several members of a working group write a preliminary draft of the specification and publish it as an I-D. That draft stimulates discussion within the working group, which may result in modifications to the draft. A second I-D is published, stimulating further discussion, which in turn results in further modifications. For successful specifications, this process continues until the group is able to agree that the current version of the draft is ready to be published as an RFC.

Not all I-Ds become RFCs, however. Some may languish due to lack of interest. Others may be dropped when some other specification appears to solve the problem better. Some never achieve a stable form.

When the IESG receives a recommendation for a standards action, it may consult with experts to review the recommendation. When the IESG is reviewing a document, it issues a *last call* notification to the IETF through the IETF-announce mailing list. Anyone may subscribe to this mailing list, and anyone may submit comments on the specification being reviewed. Once the specification is received from the working group, the last call period must be at least two weeks, but the IESG has the option of extending the last call period if it deems it necessary.

Although the IETF working group's recommendation carries weight with the IESG, it is far from binding. The IESG can even decide to consider a standards action different from that requested by the working group. Once the last call period is over, the IESG makes its decision and announces it through the IETF announce mailing list. If approved, the IESG then notifies the RFC Editor that the I-D should be withdrawn and republished as an RFC.

The Standards Track

Each time a specification is promoted to one of the three maturity levels of the Internet standards track—proposed standard, draft standard, and standard—it must go through the IESG approval process noted previously. This section examines the stated criteria for promotion to each level as described in RFC 2026. Specifications must remain at the proposed and draft standard maturity levels for minimum periods of time, but these minimums are precisely that: absolute minimums. Advancement along the standards track can be quite slow. Rather than quickly advance a specification, the IESG and IETF working groups prefer that the standard is correct rather than risk enshrining a flawed standard.

It is not uncommon for a proposed or draft standard to fail to advance on the standards track but to remain important for the Internet. For example, the Boot Protocol (BOOTP), documented in RFC 951 in 1985, is still a draft standard in 1999. Likewise, the IP Security Architecture, documented in RFC 2401 in November 1998, is still a proposed standard even though it replaces an earlier standards-track version documented by RFC 1825, published in 1995. When a specification stalls at some point in the standards track for two years, the IESG reviews the

specification every year. The IESG may subsequently decide to termi-
nate the effort or else decide that development of the specification
should continue. At the same time, the IESG may determine that the
specification itself is no longer relevant and should be reclassified as a
historical RFC rather than a standard-track specification.

As specifications advance, they are usually modified. These modifications usually require the publication of new RFCs to document the new
versions of the specification. Though it may not be necessary to repub-
lish a specification when it changes maturity level (that is, the specification is unchanged), in most cases when a specification advances, a new
RFC is published to reflect changes. If the modifications made during
the revision process are sufficiently extensive, the IESG can decide the
specification should go back and restart the process.

Proposed Standard

According to RFC 2026, to become a proposed standard, a specification
"is generally stable, has resolved known design choices, is believed to
be well-understood, has received significant community review, and
appears to enjoy enough community interest to be considered valuable." However, more experience with the specification might prove
otherwise—the specification might not be valuable, or have support, be
well-understood, or even stable—in which case the specification could
lose its status as a proposed standard.

No operational experience or even an implementation is necessary
for a specification to achieve the proposed standard level, though both
of those are helpful to a specification's cause. If the specification is likely
to have a significant impact on the Internet as it exists now, the IESG
will very likely require that the specification be implemented and
deployed.

Proposed standards are to be considered immature, but RFC 2026
encourages implementers to use the specification to build up a body of
experience that can be drawn upon to judge the protocol's value.

A specification must spend at least six months as a draft standard
before it can advance along the standards track.

Draft Standard

"A specification from which at least two independent and interoperable
implementations from different code bases have been developed, and for
which sufficient successful operational experience has been obtained,

may be elevated to the 'Draft Standard' level." That's how RFC 2026 puts it. Interoperable means that the implementations are "functionally equivalent or interchangeable." To qualify, the implementations have to implement the entire specification. If some functions or options are left out, the implementation doesn't count, unless the things that were left out of the implementations are also taken out of the specification.

Where a proposed standard should be generally stable, draft standard specifications "must be well-understood and known to be quite stable." It is up to the working group chair to document the specification's implementations, as well as to document interoperability test results and function/option support test results as a part of the chair's recommendation for moving the proposed standard to draft standard status.

Once a specification achieves draft standard status, it stays there for at least four months. This period must include an IETF meeting, so this period may be extended if the next IETF meeting occurs more than four months from the date the specification achieves draft standard.

Once a specification attains the draft standard maturity level, it is considered a final specification, one that implementers are encouraged to deploy in production systems. Although the draft standard specification may be subject to changes before attaining full standard status, those changes are most likely to be limited to fixes for specific problems arising from continued experience with the specification.

Internet Standard

According to RFC 2026, Internet standard status is reserved for specifications with "significant implementation and successful operational experience." Standards are differentiated from other maturity levels by "a high degree of technical maturity and by a generally held belief that the specified protocol or service provides significant benefit to the Internet community."

Once a specification is approved as a standard, it is assigned an STD number (see Chapter 3). Most specifications have yet to reach standard level; as of early 1999, only 56 STD numbers have ever been assigned out of almost 2,500 RFCs published.

Revising or Retiring Existing Standards

What happens when an existing standard must be updated? The process is the same for a revision to an existing standard as for a new standard. Consider the case of IPv6, the revision to the current version of the Internet Protocol, IPv4 (see also *IPv6 Clearly Explained*, Morgan Kaufman 1999). Work on the revision began in the IPng working group in the early 1990s, with the first series of IPv6 standards-track RFCs published in 1996. Continued work resulted in new versions of the IPv6 specifications, published in RFCs by late 1998 and early 1999. At the same time, the IPv4 standards are still standards and are likely to remain standards as long as IPv4 is widely implemented and deployed. When two versions of the same protocol coexist, it is necessary to document how the two versions are related.

What happens when a revised protocol replaces the older version? The revised protocol must go through the same process, and the older version may be retired unless a sufficiently large installed base uses the older version. Consider the Post Office Protocol (POP): POP version 2, documented in RFC 937, was designated historical after POP version 3 became STD-53 (RFC 1939).

Sometimes a standard becomes obsolete because a new protocol does the job much better. The Exterior Gateway Protocol (EGP), documented in RFC 904, was once STD-18. However, other routing protocols have come to replace EGP as a core protocol for the Internet, and it has since been relegated to the status of historic protocol.

Resolving Problems

One of the stated goals of the Internet standards process is to be fair, and that requires mechanisms for resolving disputes over how the process is conducted. RFC 2026 sets out guidelines for resolving problems that occur within working groups as well as problems relating to the entire standards process. These are largely common sense, at least in an organizational framework.

Although two types of disagreements are considered for working group disputes, only a single set of guidelines is provided. The types of disagreements are divided between those where an individual believes that his or her views were not given adequate consideration by the working group and those where the individual believes that the working group made an incorrect choice that could result in harm to the group's results. The resolution process relies on discussing the problem first with the working group chair or chairs, who may involve others in the group as necessary. If the problem can not be resolved at that level, it can be escalated to the area director responsible for that working group; further escalation progresses to the full IESG, and finally to the court of last resort, the IAB.

If an individual disagrees with an action taken by the IESG, the process is similar, but starts with the IESG chair. From there, the problem may be escalated to the entire IESG and then to the IAB. The IAB can not change the IESG's decision, but suggests alternatives or directs that the IESG's decision be annulled and consideration of the matter started over.

In the event that the disagreement pertains to whether the procedure itself is sufficient and fair, as described in RFC 2026, an individual can petition the board of the Internet Society.

Documenting the Process

All the groups involved in doing standards work are expected to make public their activities. This means that IETF and working group meetings must be announced on the IETF-announce mailing list. It also means that the IETF, the IESG, the IAB, all IETF working groups, and the Internet Society board must all make public their charters, minutes of their standards-related meetings, archives of working group mailing lists, and anything contributed in writing from participants in the standards process. Even expired I-Ds are archived by the IETF secretariat so as to maintain an historical record of standards activities.

IETF Workgroups

IETF working groups are designed to foster cooperation among individuals who work in widely disparate environments, from academic researchers to for-profit product developers. Working groups are also likely to include individuals who work for organizations with conflicting goals, incorporating people who work for competing software, hardware, and service vendors. Further complicating matters, working group members may live and work almost anywhere in the world.

Despite these difficulties, the bulk of the work of the IETF is accomplished by its working groups. RFC 2418 is appropriately titled "IETF Working Group Guidelines and Procedures." Describing how the working groups fit into the standards process while also outlining how successful working groups achieve their goals, this RFC should be required reading not only for anyone interested in the Internet standards process but also for anyone interested in organizational dynamics.

Defining the Working Group

An IETF working group is usually formed for the purpose of solving some specific problem or to create some specific result or results. For example, the Calendaring and Scheduling working group is chartered to "create standards that make calendaring and scheduling software significantly more useful and to enable a new class of solutions to be built that are only viable if open standards exist" (from the Calendaring and Scheduling working group charter, at www.ietf.org/html .charters/calsch-charter.html). The charter goes on to define three specific sets of problems relating to Internet calendaring and scheduling applications.

Working group deliverables are usually in the form of specifications, guidelines, or other reports published as RFCs. Once all tasks are completed, the working group may be disbanded or its operations may be suspended, with periodic review of standards as they progress through the standards track.

In keeping with the IETF's openness, IETF working groups are open to participation by anyone who wishes to contribute. Although much of the working groups' work is accomplished by small central cores of group members, other members can contribute through participation in working group mailing lists or by attending meetings in person. Again, inclusiveness reigns: Any activity that occurs at a physical meeting is reported to the mailing list, and rough consensus of the entire group is always a requirement. The working group chair can restrict contributions from members deemed to be acting counter to the interest of the group. If someone holds up meetings by discussing matters that are not appropriate or raising issues that are counter to the rough consensus, that person may be restricted from speaking, but not from attending the meeting.

There must be at least one working group chair, but usually no more than two. The chair's concern is to make "forward progress through a fair and open process" (from RFC 2418). It is up to the chair to ensure that the working group is accomplishing the tasks it is chartered to complete and nothing more or less. Other working group chair tasks include moderating the working group email list, planning working group sessions, communicating the results of the sessions, managing the work by motivating participants to do what needs to be done, developing and publishing supporting documents, and keeping track of implementations based on the working group's activities. Of course, this is a lot of work, and the chair may delegate some or all of these tasks.

Other working group staff include the secretary, who is responsible for taking minutes and recording working group decisions, and the document editor, who is responsible for ensuring that the documents the group generates truly reflect the decisions that have been made by the group. A working group facilitator, responsible for making sure that the group processes are working, may also be part of the group. The facilitator works on the style of interaction among the group members, rather than the content, to keep the group moving toward its goals. Finally, in certain cases, the IETF Area Director may assign a working group consultant to a working group. The consultant's role is to provide the benefit of his or her experience and technical expertise to the working group.

Working group members are likely to be called upon to serve on a design team. When a problem needs solving, the group may determine that a subset of the group should form a design team to solve it. Design teams can be completely informal, consisting of whoever happens to be standing around during a hallway chat, or they may be formally designated groups appointed by the working group chair to address some controversial issue, or something in between.

Working group guidelines are truly guidelines, and the working group chair is accorded considerable latitude in terms of how the working group's goals are to be achieved. As long as the process is fair and open and meets the basic requirements set forth in RFC 2418, the working group controls its own process.

A working group can be created only when certain conditions are met, and those conditions help define what working groups actually are able to do. The next section explains this process.

Creating a Working Group

Working groups are created at the behest of an IETF Area Director or by some other individual or group. The Area Director has to get behind the idea for the new group, although the IESG (with advice from the IAB) has the final say over whether the group is formed. The Area Director considers the following criteria before making any decision about pushing forward with the chartering process. These criteria help define what a working group should be, inasmuch as any existing working group should meet most if not all of them:

Clarity and relevance to the Internet community. Is there a clear vision of what the working group should be working on, and will the working group be working on something that is of value to the Internet community? Without clear goals and relevance, a proposed working group is unlikely to be chartered.

Specific and achievable goals. The working group should have specific goals that can be attained within a reasonable period of time. Working groups are meant to have finite lifetimes, and they are meant to actually perform complete tasks.

Risks and urgency. What happens if the working group is not formed? What risks are incurred if no action is taken, and what risks might be incurred if action *is* taken? Working groups that target problems that hinder Internet scalability and continued growth may get priority treatment.

Overlap with existing working groups. Will the proposed working group's activities duplicate efforts being made by any existing working groups? Will the proposed working group be working on the same or similar problems being addressed by any existing working groups? Overlap may not be bad if the new working group approaches the problem from a different technical direction. However, if only a limited number of qualified people are working on the problem, multiple working groups could cause those people's efforts to be spread a bit thin.

Interest level. Enough people must be interested in doing the work of the working group, as well as in participating as working group staff (that is, working group chair, secretary, and so on). According to RFC 2418, a viable working group requires that at least four or five people be interested in the management of the group and at least one to two dozen others must be willing to participate to the extent of attending meetings and contributing to the mailing list. The RFC also notes that the group membership must be broadly based. It is not sufficient for membership to represent a single organization, which would be viewed as an attempt by that organization to create its own Internet standard.

Expertise level. Are there enough people within the IETF who are sufficiently knowledgeable about the working group work to make worthwhile contributions, and are enough of those people interested in participating? Again, the objective of the working group is to accomplish specific objectives. If the working group members aren't experienced in the technologies they are working with, it's unlikely they'll be able to achieve those goals.

End-user interest level. Is there a consumer base for the output of the working group? Are end users interested in seeing the goals proposed by the working group charter accomplished? The IETF is an engineering organization, whose production is intended for use by end users. Pure-research projects are better accomplished by the IRTF; the IETF must concern itself with products that have practical applications.

Practicality of IETF involvement. All the criteria listed here might be met, but some specifications are better produced by other bodies. There may be interest, expertise, relevance, and all the rest, but the IETF is unlikely to get involved with developing standards for LAN media or object models. Other bodies are better qualified to produce specifications in these areas.

Intellectual property rights issues. Increasingly, intellectual property rights—software patents, copyrights, and more—are relevant to work being done by working groups. These issues must be understood before the working group is chartered.

Open technology. Many organizations would like to have their proprietary standards recognized as Internet standards. Such recognition would accord the organization a significant advantage over competitors. When evaluating applications for new working groups, the IESG must attempt to determine whether the work planned by the group is an attempt to favor some existing, closed technology, or whether the plan is devised to solicit IETF participation to genuinely develop an open specification.

Understanding of the technologies and issues. Are the issues and technologies proposed for the working group's activities well understood? Technologies should be reasonably mature before they are brought into an Internet standards effort. The IESG would prefer to avoid the kind of debacle that could result from rushing into unproven technology.

Overlap with other standards bodies. Do the working group's goals intersect with the goals of any other standards bodies? This may not be cause for concern if the working group approaches the issues in a way unique for the Internet, but the IESG would have to evaluate the degree to which liaison with the other group exists or is required.

Once the Area Director is satisfied that a working group proposal is in good shape, the chartering process starts. The Area Director and the person who is to become the working group chair work out the charter together and then submit it to the IESG for approval and to the IAB for review. The charter includes a description of the working group and its objectives and goals, scheduled milestones necessary to achieve those goals, and a list of administrative details like names and contact information for working group chair(s).

Working Group Operations

Working groups have a certain amount of latitude in how they operate, as long as the procedures that result are open and fair. Most of the action usually takes place on the mailing list, with members of the group suggesting options, debating the value of different approaches, and discussing problems arising from implementation and deployment of the solutions being considered by the working group.

The standard for moving working group tasks forward is rough consensus, meaning that most of the group is mostly agreed about the solution in question. Determining where the rough consensus actually is, is the job of the working group chair. This can be difficult when all work is carried on over the mailing list, but it is certainly possible. Consensus can also be determined at meetings, where the group can vote in some way. In either case, when the chair feels that a consensus has been reached, the chair may solicit comments from the list or call for a vote. No hard and fast rule determines where consensus actually lies in terms of how many are in favor and how many opposed: The only guideline provided in RFC 2418 is that agreement by 51 percent of the group is not enough to form a rough consensus, and when the group is 99 percent in agreement, a more than rough consensus definitely does exist.

Working Group Documentation

First and foremost, the raw activity of the working group is available in the archives for the working group mailing list. Here you will find all the comments, arguments, proposals, and questions raised in the group. You will also find agendas for physical meetings, meeting minutes, and notifications about the publication of other working group documents, particularly Internet-Drafts and RFCs. Anyone interested in the output of a particular IETF working group should subscribe to the mailing list right away.

For a more formal look at the results of the work of a working group, look at the Internet-Drafts it generates. Although these are definitely working documents, they do reflect the best and most recent version of the working group's product. An I-D may be revised many times before it is finally approved and published as an RFC, but only one version of the I-D is ever publicly available at any given time. To trace the development of a specification across time, you must either follow the mailing list or download and store copies of each new revision of the I-D. However, most I-D revisions include a section detailing the changes made since the previous version.

The ultimate documentation of a working group's activity is the finished RFCs it generates. An I-D is just a draft, and six months after it is published, it expires unless it can be moved forward. RFCs, on the other hand, live forever and contain information that is at least of some interest to the Internet community and that may actually describe a specification on the Internet standards track.

Reading List

Table 4.1 lists some RFCs that elaborate on the information presented in this chapter.

Table 4.1   Relevant RFCs

RFC	TITLE	DESCRIPTION
RFC 2026	The Internet Standards Process—Revision 3	This document serves as the basis of much of this chapter and explains the exact process by which specifications become standards.
RFC 2418	IETF Working Group Guidelines and Procedures	This document explains how working groups work, how to start one, how to run one, and how to terminate one.
RFC 2028	Organizations Involved in the IETF Standards Process	This RFC explains what organizational entities are involved in the process of setting standards, as well as what roles each plays.

Table 4.1   *(Continued)*

RFC	TITLE	DESCRIPTION
RFC 1796	Not All RFCs Are Standards	This short RFC simply punctuates the distinction between acceptance of a specification as a standard and acceptance of a specification for publication as an RFC.
RFC 2223	Instructions to RFC Authors	This RFC is useful for anyone wishing to write an RFC or RFC-like document as well as for those interested in how these documents are styled and structured.

Getting the RFCs

You can find RFCs in lots of places, though some are more complete, accurate, and up-to-date than others. In this chapter, we examine where to find RFCs and Internet-Drafts, and where to get the latest information about RFCs and Internet-Drafts.

RFCs can be found almost everywhere, it seems. Computer book authors have been known to include complete copies of RFCs in their books, and some authors incorporate searchable databases of RFCs on CD-ROMs included with their books. Yahoo! may have as many as a dozen or so RFC-related sites, most of which are archives containing all (or almost all) RFCs published to date. I've included a handful of the Web archive sites I find most useful, and you can find more pointers on the companion Web site for this book. However, anyone interested in getting the latest should do his or her own search for RFC-related Web sites: Old ones go away, new ones come online all the time, and the ones that stay on often undergo changes, sometimes for the better and sometimes for the worse.

Having all the RFCs does not necessarily give you everything you need to work with RFCs, however. For one thing, there are somewhere in the neighborhood of 2,500 different RFCs. Trying to find what you need in that thicket of documents is sort of like trying to find what you need in an encyclopedia whose articles are arranged in the order they were written. To make things worse, revisions of existing articles are simply treated as newer articles, and the older, outdated articles are never removed. And, of course, there is no index.

To make sense of RFCs, you need something to act as an index. In most cases, that something is a search tool associated with the Web site or CD-ROM where the RFCs themselves are published. RFC archives may be totally spartan, like the directory published by the IETF, which is nothing more than an FTP directory containing the RFC files. More elaborate archives provide tools for searching and displaying the RFCs, with varying degrees of success. So far, no single site provides everything you need to work with RFCs, but some combination of two or three should be sufficient to meet most needs.

Staying on Top of RFCs

There are several different types of RFC consumers. The more casual consumers are usually more interested in looking up some specific standard or document on a one-time or infrequent basis. A network manager may consult an RFC to check on header fields or some other aspect of a protocol while troubleshooting a network problem. Computer science students may consult the RFC archives to document some protocol. Students of history may consult the RFC archives to track down some Internet-related event. The casual reader may have been given an RFC number by a text reference (like this one), a vendor, a professor, or some other source, and thus may have no need for any type of search engine. Casual RFC readers often find out about new Internet standards-track specification from their vendors or from trade press reports about new products that support them.

People involved with deploying Internet-based or related systems may have a higher level of interest in RFCs. Intranet/extranet managers need to understand what their systems are doing and how they do it. This includes understanding the protocols as well as how vendors implement those protocols. These users need to be able to search for RFCs based on keywords. They need to be able to jump from one RFC to another related RFC to see how they affect each other. They need to know which RFC is a current standard (or nonstandard) and which is obsolete or experimental.

These readers may even need to know when a new specification has been added to the standards track or when an existing specification advances along the standards track.

The third class of RFC readers are those who not only need access to current RFCs, but who must know what future RFCs will look like. These are the implementers—network software and hardware engineers who must translate the specifications from document form into products that actually do something. Not only must these implementers know when new specifications are published as RFCs or advanced along the standards track, but they must have a pretty good idea of where the specification is going well before it is published as an RFC. Vendors implement specifications described in Internet-Drafts for experimentation and testing so they can roll out RFC-compliant products quickly once the RFC is published.

This book was written for people in the two latter categories, and in the next section we look at some of the more important mailing lists to which you should subscribe if you need timely information about RFCs.

IETF Mailing Lists

Several mailing lists are worth knowing about if you are interested in what the IETF is doing:

IETF-discuss. The IETF discussions list is an open forum for IETF members to discuss issues related to the Internet, the IETF, the IESG, and their activities. If you are considering subscribing to this list, check out the archives at the IETF Web site.

IETF-announce. The IETF announcement list is used to distribute information about the logistics of IETF meetings, agendas for IETF meetings, actions taken on working group activities, announcements of Internet-Drafts, IESG last calls, Internet standard actions, and announcements of publication of new RFCs. This is a read-only list, and it is used to communicate official activities of the IETF and IESG, rather than to stimulate discussion.

Internet Monthly Report. Subscribers to this mailing list receive copies of a monthly report detailing all the activities of participating organizations during the month preceding. In this report, you can find a summary of all standard actions, new RFCs and Internet-Drafts published, activities of the RFC editor and the IANA, information about meetings that were held during the month, and notices of relevant meetings to come.

RFC-dist. This is the RFC distribution list. Subscribers receive notification every time a new RFC is published, along with a URL pointing to the newly published document.

To avoid duplication of messages, most people would choose to subscribe to only one of the IETF-announce, RFC-dist, or Internet Monthly Report lists. For example, if you want notification every time a new RFC is published but are not interested in Internet-Drafts or any other Internet actions, you would subscribe to the RFC-dist list. If you don't want to be bombarded with messages but still want to stay on top of Internet standards activities, you would subscribe to the Internet Monthly Report. If you need to know everything that happens, as it happens, you would subscribe to the IETF-announce list. All RFC-dist list messages are copied to the IETF-announce list, as is the Internet Monthly Report, so subscribing to the IETF-announce list is the most comprehensive option.

Table 5.1 includes subscription information for these lists as well URLs for list archives. Before subscribing, readers are urged to visit the archive sites listed in Table 5.1 and read all instructions about the mailing list before subscribing.

Table 5.1   Addresses for Subscribing to IETF-related Mailing Lists

MAILING LIST	EMAIL ADDRESS	ARCHIVE SITE	NOTES
RFC-dist	majordomo@ zephyr.isi.edu	(included in IETF announce list archive)	Message body should read "subscribe rfc-dist".
IETF-announce	ietf-announce-request@ietf.org	www.ietf.org/mail-archive/ietf-announce/maillist.html	Use "subscribe" as both the subject line and the message body.
Internet Monthly Report	majordomo@ isi.edu	ftp://ftp.isi.edu/ in-notes/imr/	Message body should read "subscribe imr".
IETF Discussion List	ietf-request@ ietf.org	www.ietf.org/mail-archive/ietf/maillist.html	Use "subscribe" as both the subject line and the message body.

NOTE The IETF discussion list can be very noisy at times—it is an open forum from which no one may be ejected and without any type of censorship. Participants sometimes veer off onto topics not relevant to the IETF, post repetitively on the same topic, or return to topics that are no longer relevant or that have already been discussed into the ground. An alternative exists for people who are busy and want to know what's being discussed, without the cross-postings, postings from known troublemakers, and repeated requests for help in unsubscribing. The *ietf+censored* list filters out much of the noise and can be subscribed to by sending a message to *ietf+censored-request@alvestrand.no* with the body "*subscribe.*"

For those interested in seeing only the rejected messages (for amusement purposes only), send a message body of *subscribe* to the address *ietf+censored-rejects-request@alvestrand.no.*

For more information about these lists, see *www.alvestrand.no/ietf+censored.html.*

RFC Archives

Dozens of RFC archives scattered over the globe exist on the Internet. Some are more useful than others, and some are better than others. The RFC archive on the IETF site contains the raw RFCs as text files and, in some cases, as PostScript files. However, this is simply a file transfer site: There are no search tools here. If you need help with RFCs, you need to find another resource.

Rather than list all the RFC archives currently available, this section discusses how to locate archives and what kinds of features are available in RFC archives. Links to some of the better RFC archives are available on the companion Web site to this book; readers are urged to make their own search for a source that is appropriate for them.

Finding RFC Archives

Locating an RFC archive on the Internet is relatively simple. Try the RFC editor Web site for a list of some RFC archives:

www.rfc-editor.org/rfc.html

This is a good place to start because it describes some of the features and capabilities of the listed sites.

Portal sites like Yahoo! also maintain categories related to Internet standards. Yahoo! even has a category just for RFCs (http://dir.yahoo .com/Computers_and_Internet/Standards/RFCs/), which is a fertile hunting ground for RFC archive sites. Portals may offer more selection, including off-beat archive sites.

If you don't find what you want at a portal site, you can try one of the Web search sites like AltaVista, HotBot, or others. A search on the word "RFC" will undoubtedly produce thousands of matches, but you can narrow it down by adding qualifying words such as "archive," "search," or "standards." You may also be able to narrow the search down to geographic areas or languages: HotBot offers criteria based on domain, continent, and language as well as the more common Boolean searches on words.

RFC Archive Features

RFC archives usually offer a mix of features, and some mixtures are more useful than others. Some archives are simply that: repositories for raw RFC files. If you know the RFC number, you can use these archives; if not, you may be out of luck. Some of these file dumps actually list the RFC names, authors, and date of publication in addition to the number, so you can use your browser's search function to find relevant documents as long as you know what to look for.

At a minimum, the archive should provide a search function. Searching should be done on the body of the RFC text, rather than just on RFC titles. Some archives' searches are too restrictive and produce way too few hits; other archives' searches are too loose and produce way too many hits. The "just right" number of hits varies from person to person, but the search results should include all the relevant RFCs without including too many irrelevant ones.

Consider too the search features. Some archives permit only simple searches on one or more terms; others permit Boolean text searches. Some archives allow you to fine-tune your searches, limiting the number of hits; others restrict you to a maximum number of hits and urge you to add terms if you exceed that maximum. Some allow complex searches with criteria relating to the title and body of the RFCs, as well as options regarding the output of the results. The more control you have over the search, the more likely you are to find just the documents you want.

Some archive sites include only RFCs, while others provide access to Internet-Drafts as well. Likewise, some archive sites allow you to search or browse through document subsets, such as the STD, BCP, and FYI series of RFCs.

Finally, some sites even include hyperlinking: RFCs (and possibly other documents) cited in the body of the RFC you are reading are activated at Web links. Open up one RFC, and you can immediately jump to any RFC cited in the text by clicking on it. This is a great idea, but the implementations tend to fall short. The RFC being displayed usually links to itself through the RFC number listed in the page headers. One version actually seems to link any number with three or more digits, including zip codes and binary values of fields included in protocol descriptions.

RFCs by Email

For those with email-only access to the Internet, RFCs are available by email from the RFC-INFO service. Send email to rfc-info@isi.edu and format your message body like this:

Retrieve: RFC

Doc-ID: RFC####

Replace #### with the number of the RFC you want, padding the value with zeros for RFC numbers that are lower than 1000. For example, to retrieve RFC 821, you would use *RFC0821*.

For additional features or for help with retrieving RFCs by email, you can send a message to rfc-info@isi.edu with the message body *help: help*.

Getting Internet-Drafts

Subscribing to the IETF-announce mailing list will get you, among other things, announcements of publication of all new I-Ds. These announcements include URLs you can use to retrieve a copy of the I-D. You may also want to search for I-Ds that relate to a particular technology or issue.

You can see all I-Ds generated by a particular IETF working group at the active working group Web page:

www.ietf.org/html.charters/wg-dir.html

Choose the working group of interest from this list, and you'll see all its RFCs and I-Ds. Many related organizations also maintain archives of I-Ds as well as RFCs; for example, the Internet Mail Consortium maintains RFCs and I-Ds related to Internet mail at its Web site:

www.imc.org/mail-standards.html

The IETF maintains the most up-to-date and comprehensive list of I-Ds. The main repository for Internet-Drafts is at:

www.ietf.org/ID.html

From this page, you can do a keyword search, browse through the I-D directory, or view guidelines for I-D authors. Many of the other good RFC repositories also include facilities for searching for I-Ds.

Reading List

Rather than suggest any specific references for additional reading in this chapter, you should go to your favorite Web search or portal site to search for RFC archives. If you can't find at least five, try another search engine. Now, try each of the archive sites you've located and see which one best suits you.

Regardless of whether you do your own search, be sure to visit Lynn Wheeler's IETF RFC Index site (www.garlic.com/~lynn/rfcietf.html). It is one of the most comprehensive and useful archives around. Wheeler provides the ability to view specifications at different stages of the standards track as well as view-only specific document series. Also included here are links to specifications that have been made obsolete as well as the specifications that have replaced them. Links to related sites are also useful.

Reading the RFCs

As mentioned in Chapter 5, "Getting the RFCs," RFC consumers tend to fall into three categories: casual readers, deployers, and developers. Just as each type of consumer has slightly different requirements for obtaining and tracking RFCs and Internet-Drafts, so too does each type of consumer use these documents in a different way. This chapter takes a look at how people use RFCs.

Though it may not be apparent from reading some of the earlier RFCs, new Internet documents must conform to a very specific set of stylistic requirements. RFC 2223, "Instructions to RFC Authors," is a must-read for anyone who plans to write an Internet-Draft or RFC. It is also useful for understanding just what is and is not included in an RFC.

All RFCs are published as ASCII text files because it is a universal format, accessible to anyone with email or better Internet access. Occasionally an RFC may also be published in PostScript to provide additional detail to graphics included in the document, but most ASCII RFCs include text-based graphics. All modern RFCs adhere to a strict page format, with headers that contain the RFC number, title, and month and year of publication and footers that contain the author(s), RFC category (informational, standards-track, best current practices, or experimental), and page number. The first page displays the RFC number, the authors' names, their organizational affiliation, and a line indicating which previous RFCs the current one updates or makes obsolete. If the document has any other numbers, for example an STD, FYI, or BCP number, these are listed at the top of the first page as well.

RFCs must have a status section, identifying the RFC as documenting a standards track specification, a best current practice (BCP), an experimental specification, or an informational document. The status section consists of one of four boilerplate paragraphs, each one indicating a different type of document. A brief boilerplate copyright notice, reserving copyright for the Internet Society, is also required on the first page, with a longer piece of boilerplate added at the end of the document.

The introduction section briefly describes the document itself. This section is often the most useful when the reader is searching for a particular specification. The introduction summarizes the RFC, usually in a few paragraphs or less. The introduction section is usually derived from the abstract section of its precursor Internet-Draft.

Other required sections for RFCs include a references section citing all previously published documents to which the RFC refers and a security considerations section discussing potential security issues raised by the RFC. The author's address section is also required, as it permits readers to send questions or comments directly to the author.

Of course, these sections are the shell within which the meat of the RFC is nestled. After the introduction, the specification is described in detail. The first section after the introduction often describes pertinent terminology and may be followed by a section or sections describing the requirements or circumstances that caused the specification to be written. The protocol headers and fields are then described, followed by discussion of specific protocol features and how they work. The last sections may discuss how the protocol interacts with other protocols, how it should be implemented or deployed, or any other issues that need to be addressed in order to implement the protocol. Appendices are often used where appropriate.

RFCs usually describe behaviors and attributes of protocols. They tell you how a system using the protocol should work. From there, you can build your own implementation of the protocol. RFCs don't usually explain how to build the implementations, they just tell you how an implementation would work if it were built. Some RFCs describe protocol

APIs, but these still describe how the implementations must behave rather than how to actually program the implementations.

Understanding Protocols

Perhaps the most common use of RFCs is to understand what the protocol being specified actually does and how it works. Casual readers as well as developers must first look to the RFC for a basic understanding before anything else can happen. Casual readers may be able to stop there, although both deployers and developers need to look beyond a basic understanding of the specification to meet their needs.

Getting a basic understanding of a protocol may be as simple as reading the introduction section of the RFC; this is often all that is necessary. However, things are not always that simple. Sometimes it is necessary to read through the entire RFC, and even then the answer may not be apparent. In those cases, it may be worthwhile to check on the citations in the RFC reference section as well as any related or dependent specifications. When all else fails, the casual reader may need to take a short course in TCP/IP internetworking.

Reading the RFCs

Always start with the introduction. This usually is the most precise and concise summary of the specification available anywhere. The introduction usually explains what the protocol does and how it does it. You can often rule out an RFC as being irrelevant by looking at the introduction. You may also determine that a protocol does what you want it to do, the way you want to do it, by reading the introduction.

More often, you will need to delve further into the RFC to find what you need. Sometimes you will have to pay careful attention to the definitions section, especially if the specification refers to systems or processes with which you are unfamiliar. Sometimes the definitions will be mostly formalized descriptions of terms that are well understood. Read any sections that discuss the background of the problem that the specification solves or attempts to solve. This section may describe not only the approach used by the specification described in the RFC but also other competitive or precursor solutions.

Most casual readers will have found their answer by now. Most of the basics of the protocol and its special features are outlined in the first few sections of the RFC; reading beyond that into the protocol nitty-gritty of headers and detailed specifications may not provide answers to simple questions. At this point, it may be useful to look at references and protocol dependencies rather than attempting to divine further meaning from the RFC in question.

Checking References and Dependencies

If the reader simply wants to understand the broad outlines of the protocol, sometimes more background is needed rather than more detail about the specification being examined. Internet protocol specifications often expand as they are updated, especially as they progress along the standards track. A specification that is sufficient for a proposed standard usually expands over time as people uncover potential problems or issues related to the deployment of the protocol on the Internet. RFCs of updated protocols tend to expand in order to deal with, or at least acknowledge, these issues and problems.

To understand the basic concepts of a revised specification, it is sometimes useful to go back to the original specification. Likewise, documents cited in the references section often include discussions of the issues and approaches and concepts used as background for development of the specification described in the RFC. Often, the documents are other RFCs or Internet-Drafts and are easily accessible online.

An RFC can specify a new version, update, or replacement for an existing specification. For example, when a proposed standard has been revised and moved to draft standard status, the new version is given a new RFC number. However, just looking at the original, proposed standard RFC will not give you any indication that the RFC has been deprecated. Relations between RFCs are indicated in Lynn Wheeler's RFC Web site (www.garlic.com/~lynn/rfcietf.html).

Getting More Help

When reading the RFC doesn't help and the references are similarly unenlightening, the casual reader may need more internetworking background. Books like *TCP/IP Clearly Explained, 3rd edition* (Pete Loshin, Morgan Kaufman 1999) or *Illustrated TCP/IP* (Matthew Naugle, Wiley 1998) provide general readers with enough background to begin to read RFCs with greater understanding of the basic concepts of internetworking.

Alternatively, casual readers can often find answers to technical questions, or at least pointers to good sources for such answers, on mailing lists and newsgroups devoted to the protocol specified in the RFC. Public newsgroups are available for most Internet protocols, as are FAQs for those groups. Mailing lists maintained by the relevant IETF working group are often helpful, though the reader is still urged to check the list archives or read a few days' worth of newsgroup postings to see what kinds of questions are encouraged and to see whether the question has recently been answered.

RFC Troubleshooting

From "what does this protocol do?" to "why doesn't this protocol work?" is a big step. Deployers of protocols need to be able to read the specifications with a more critical eye than most casual readers. They need to understand not only how to identify which protocol is at fault and how protocols behave, but also how to look at network traffic and determine what is actually going on.

Casual readers often know exactly what protocol and even what RFC they should be looking for: They may have been told that a certain specification solves their problems or is incorporated into a new networking product they are considering for purchase. Troubleshooters have no such assurances. More often, the people involved with troubleshooting products that have been deployed know only that some system is not working as they believe it should be working. They must first analyze the problem and rule out the more commonplace causes before they need to examine the protocol specifications.

Protocol analysis tools capture and decode network traffic. Network managers can examine protocol behaviors by looking at the traffic being sent and received by local systems. Initial descriptions of network problems usually are phrased in terms of lack of connectivity between systems or failure of system functions despite apparent connectivity. The solution usually lies in something external to the protocol, or at least in some issue relating to the installation or configuration of the protocol implementation.

Network support staff are usually able to solve problems through the process of elimination: Misconfigured systems, disabled servers, or overly strict firewalls account for a large portion of these problems. Network engineers using protocol analyzers can eliminate the peskier problems that relate to protocol implementations by studying the actual network transmissions and determining whether the implementations are behaving as they are supposed to.

Problems with implementations can also be tracked down by replacing the problem system or systems with other systems known to work correctly. Scanning network transmissions, the engineers can determine whether the functionally equivalent systems are actually behaving in the same ways. Even though Internet standards are well defined, as are the requirements for implementing them, not all implementations are created equal. An implementation may be incomplete or incorrect either through design or in error, but to detect a problem you must understand what the implementation is supposed to do, as defined in the relevant RFC.

Deployment professionals who are reading RFCs for troubleshooting purposes must be able to go beyond the basics of the specification and understand the specific functions defined by the protocol. Thus, it is not enough to understand that TCP, for example, uses four different timing functions to guarantee service across a virtual circuit. You must also understand exactly how those timers are supposed to work and why performance can be disrupted if one or more of them is improperly implemented.

Newsgroups and mailing lists are far more important tools for the deployment professional than the casual RFC reader, as they are sources of information about specific implementations as well as good places to ask technical questions. Whereas basic questions about a protocol are less welcome in such forums, issues about how protocol implementations actually work are central to the operation of the IETF working groups as well as to participants on newsgroups and mailing lists.

Building Protocol Implementations

No one has a greater need to be on top of the Internet standards process than the people responsible for building the applications that implement standard protocols. Any implementer who waits for a specification to achieve full Internet standard status loses all hope of ever attaining significant market share without huge cost. This is what happened to Microsoft when it first started building Internet software. Microsoft started building its Web browser long after Netscape and Spyglass dominated the market. Ultimately, Microsoft garnered significant share only by giving away its browser and by bundling it into as many products and packages as it could manage. In effect, Microsoft had to start from scratch in order to catch up; in fact, Microsoft licensed browser code from Spyglass before building its own browser.

Having learned from experience, Microsoft now participates in many IETF working groups. Not only does Microsoft gain access to valuable information about what the new and revised standards will look like, but it also guides those efforts through the working groups.

If you want to implement a protocol for a commercial product or service, you are not alone. If you want your product to succeed, it must be timely, and that means, at the least, tracking protocol development from the Internet-Draft phase. Ideally, protocol implementers actively participate in the standards development process through working group mailing lists and by attending working group meetings.

Understanding the Standards

The relevant protocol is not always immediately apparent, nor is there only a single relevant protocol for a particular application. A developer working on collaborative workgroup software may be affected by specifications relating to Internet messaging, calendaring and scheduling, IP multicast, multimedia data transmission, and quality of service. Switch and router developers must stay abreast of all developments relating to IP routing as well as to data link layer transports like Ethernet, ATM, Frame Relay, FDDI, and others.

Understanding the standards means not just reading the relevant RFCs and Internet-Drafts, but also looking at existing implementations. The IETF maintains reports on implementations of Internet standards (at www.ietf.org/IESG/implementation.html). Prospective implementers are advised to start here by looking at existing implementations and reports about those implementations (there is some talk of enhancing the IETF's role in making reference implementations of standard protocols available).

It's important to remember that by working within the system, implementers have access to far more information and assistance than is incorporated into the RFCs.

Reading List

The best way to get comfortable with reading RFCs is by simply reading an RFC that covers a topic that is of interest. In addition to the RFCs listed in previous chapters, you can use your preferred mechanism to search for an RFC on some aspect of ATM, and then simply try to make sense of it.

As you read, try to answer some questions:

- What kind of RFC is it? (e.g., informational, standards track, etc.)

- Does the RFC belong to some other document series? (e.g., BCP, STD, FYI, etc.)

- Is there any way you can use the RFC to confirm that a behavior or characteristic of some familiar application or system complies with the RFC?

- Can you locate any of the RFC's references, to gain greater insight into the RFC you just read?

All of these exercises should help you master the art of reading RFCs.

Network Management Fundamentals

The Simple Network Management Protocol (SNMP) uses a very clever architecture for monitoring and managing network devices, services, functions, and performance. The SNMP architecture relies on what is, in effect, a vastly distributed database. Every monitored device stores information about itself in a rigorously structured format, conforming to a database schema called a Management Information Base (MIB). MIBs consist of objects and events that are defined using a Structure of Management Information (SMI). SNMP defines a set of rules for management applications to access the information stored in a MIB and to modify that information when and where appropriate.

Different MIBs are defined for different types of systems. Any device connected to an IP network is required to maintain a certain minimum required set of information pertaining to IP nodes. A device acting as a server may be required to support a different set of MIB modules in addition to the basic MIB for IP nodes. Depending on the node's network interface, additional MIB modules may be desirable.

In this chapter, we review the standards behind the SNMP network management architecture: SNMP itself, SMI, MIB. We also discuss the need for adding managed objects specific to a node's network interface. In Chapter 14, "ATM Management," we introduce the specific Internet-standard network management specifications relevant to managing nodes in an ATM network.

Internet Standard Management Framework

According to RFC 2570, "Introduction to Version 3 of the Internet-Standard Network Management Framework," any organization that uses the Internet Standard Management Framework will contain these four basic components:

Managed nodes. RFC 2570 specifies the number as "several (typically many)." A managed node contains an SNMP agent that can provide information to network management entities.

One or more SNMP managers. In other words, at least one management application can solicit or collect information from the managed nodes.

A protocol for transferring management information among SNMP entities. This refers to the Simple Network Management Protocol.

Management information. This is the information that the SNMP agents make available to SNMP managers and that the managers can use to determine things such as how much traffic is going through a particular interface or what kind of machine is connected to a particular interface.

These are the actual things that get deployed in a managed network. The things themselves are specified in conformance with (what else) a set of Internet specifications and go beyond the protocol that defines how information gets passed from a managed node to a manager. The management framework has a modular architecture that, according to RFC 2570, includes the following:

- A data definition language
- A definition of the management information
- A definition of the protocol
- Security and administration

The Structure of Management Information (SMI) provides a language for management information, while the Management Information Base (MIB) uses the SMI to define management information. The SNMP specification defines the protocol, and a series of other specifications defines the rules for network management security and administration.

Of course, all these components are defined in RFCs. Table 7.1 shows some of the documents that describe this architecture, including which part of the architecture each RFC documents. Missing from this table are the many different MIB modules: They are included in Table 7.2 and number very close to 100, with more Internet-Draft MIB modules being submitted regularly.

Table 7.1 Components of the Internet Standard Management Framework

COMPONENT	RFC	STD	TITLE
Protocol definition	1157	15	Simple Network Management Protocol (SNMP)
Data definition language	1212		Concise MIB Definitions
Definition of management information	1213		Management Information Base for Network Management of TCP/IP-based Internets: MIB-II
Protocol definition	1905		Protocol Operations for Version 2 of the Simple Network Management Protocol (SNMPv2)
Protocol definition	1906		Transport Mappings for Version 2 of the Simple Network Management Protocol (SNMPv2)
Definition of management information	1907		Management Information Base for Version 2 of the Simple Network Management Protocol (SNMPv2)
Protocol definition	2570		Introduction to Version 3 of the Internet-Standard Network Management Framework
Protocol definition	2571		An Architecture for Describing SNMP Management Frameworks
Protocol definition	2572		Message Processing and Dispatching for the Simple Network Management Protocol (SNMP)
Security and administration	2573		SNMP Applications

Continues

Table 7.1 Components of the Internet Standard Management Framework *(Continued)*

COMPONENT	RFC	STD	TITLE
Security and administration	2574		The User-Based Security Model for Version 3 of the Simple Network Management Protocol (SNMPv3)
Security and administration	2575		View-based Access Control Model for the Simple Network Management Protocol (SNMP)
Data definition language	2578	58	Structure of Management Information Version 2 (SMIv2)
Data definition language	2579	58	Textual Conventions for SMIv2
Data definition language	2580	58	Conformance Statements for SMIv2

The rest of this chapter outlines the basics of the Structure of Management Information, followed by a discussion of how that structure is used to create the Management Information Base. From there, we can summarize how the Simple Network Management Protocol works, followed by a discussion of the Interfaces Group MIB and how it all relates to ATM.

Structure of Management Information

RFC 2578, "Structure of Management Information Version 2 (SMIv2)," (Internet standard STD 58) defines the schema to be used for the database that is the Management Information Base (MIB). Using the Abstract Syntax Notation One (ASN.1), RFC 2578 defines a framework for the data to be used by network management tools through SNMP.

Although a thorough discussion of ASN.1 and database schemas is beyond the scope of this text, a figure and an example help clarify matters. The SMI defines how any particular piece of information can be expressed and identified within the structure. Every piece of information or object is identified with an object identifier value: a unique value that authoritatively names an object. Each part of the object identifier describes, in successively greater precision, what object that object identifier refers to.

The object identifier is hierarchical, so that the leftmost value in the ID is the most general. When it has a value of 0, it indicates an object administered by the CCITT (the international committee that recommends communications standards, formerly named the Comite Consultatif

Internationale de Telegraphie et Telephonie, now known as the ITU, but still referred to as the CCITT in this schema). When the value is 1, it indicates an object administered by the ISO. When the value is 2, it indicates a jointly administered object. All things Internet are ISO objects (as are many other things, by the way), so the first part of their object ID is always 1.

Under the ISO are four subordinates, numbered 0 through 3. We're interested in the identified organizations subordinate, 3, because that's where the Defense Advanced Research Projects Agency (DARPA) can be found as a subsubordinate (number 6). The Internet is number 1 under that subordinate. Thus, any Internet-related objects in this schema begin with the values:

```
1.3.6.1...
```

It doesn't stop there—for our purposes, that's very close to the beginning. As Figure 7.1 shows, the hierarchy continues down from there with several additional branches under Internet(1). As you can see, any object residing under the mib-2(1) object would be represented as:

```
1.3.6.1.2.1....
```

This structure makes it possible for one network entity (perhaps a network management application) to query another network entity

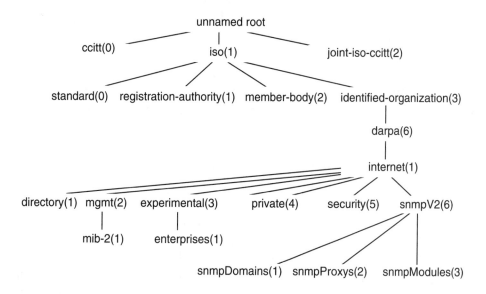

Figure 7.1 Structure of management information.

(perhaps a managed server, client workstation, or even a printer) for information stored within this structure. All managed devices have this structure built in, and thus network management applications can simply request a value for a particular node by specifying the object identifier.

There is much more to SMI, of course. For one thing, there is the Abstract Syntax Notation One (ASN.1), an ISO standard for representing data. For another, there is considerable documentation of how ASN.1 is to be used and how to format and represent data within the SMI. However, this is beyond the scope of this book.

Management Information Base

The SMI creates a framework within which to build a database. The Management Information Base (MIB) creates the actual database. Allowing each vendor to create its own management and administration database schema for each product would result in confusion: One vendor might call the field containing the number of packets processed by a router "PACKETS," while another might call it "PKTS_PROC." Instead, all vendors use the dot-delimited object representations to hold relevant data.

Originally intended to be a monolithic structure, defined by a single group, the MIB is clearly too big a task for any single entity to get its arms around. No single entity could be expected to know just what kind of information would be needed by an Ethernet hub as well as what would be needed by an ATM switch as well as what would be needed by all the other devices and servers for which MIBs have been defined. Table 7.2 shows a list of most of the RFCs defining MIBs, along with their status and standard number (where relevant). There are a lot, as you can see.

MIB specifications generally begin with a description of the problem for which they are being proposed as a solution. They also contain a complete, formal definition of the MIB components. This includes ASN.1 representation of the objects defined by the MIB, including a description of the data contained in each object.

The MIB defines what kind of data can be stored and under what object identifier. Devices supporting the MIB are not limited to one instance of any given object. For example, you might want to be able to represent a series of pieces of data all related to a particular entity. In that case, you could use a row to store the related data. You might also want to represent multiple objects containing information about network interfaces for a router or even just a series of instances of a row as in a routing table. Multiple instances of data can be stored in tables, with the table accessible through the object identifier.

Table 7.2 MIB Documents

STATUS	NAME	RFC	STD
Standard	Concise MIB Definitions	1212	16
Standard	Management Information Base-II	1213	17
Experimental	CLNS-MIB	1238	
Proposed	Border Gateway Protocol MIB (Version 3)	1269	
Proposed	FDDI-MIB	1285	
Proposed	SNMP MIB Extension for X.25 LAPB	1381	
Proposed	SNMP MIB Extension for X.25 Packet Layer	1382	
Proposed	DS1/E1 Interface Type	1406	
Proposed	DS3/E3 Interface Type	1407	
Proposed	Identification MIB	1414	
Proposed	Multiprotocol Interconnect on X.25 MIB	1461	
Proposed	Link Control Protocol of PPP MIB	1471	
Proposed	Security Protocols of PPP MIB	1472	
Proposed	IP Network Control Protocol of PPP MIB	1473	
Proposed	Bridge PPP MIB	1474	
Draft	BRIDGE-MIB	1493	
Proposed	FDDI Management Information Base	1512	
Proposed	Token Ring Extensions to RMON MIB	1513	
Proposed	Host Resources MIB	1514	
Proposed	802.3 MAU MIB	1515	
Proposed	Source Routing Bridge MIB	1525	
Draft	DECNET MIB	1559	
Proposed	X.500 Directory Monitoring MIB	1567	
Proposed	Evolution of the Interfaces Group of MIB-II Elective	1573	

Continues

Table 7.2 MIB Documents *(Continued)*

STATUS	NAME	RFC	STD
Proposed	MIB SONET/SDH Interface Type	1595	
Proposed	Frame Relay Service MIB	1604	
Proposed	DNS Server MIB Extensions	1611	
Proposed	DNS Resolver MIB Extensions	1612	
Proposed	UPS Management Information Base	1628	
Standard	Ethernet MIB	1643	50
Draft	BGP-4 MIB	1657	
Draft	Def Man Objs Character Stream	1658	
Draft	Def Man Objs RS-232-like	1659	
Draft	Def Man Objs Parallel-printer-like	1660	
Proposed	SNA NAUs MIB using SMIv2	1666	
Draft	SIP Interface Type MIB	1694	
Proposed	ATM Management Version 8.0 using SMIv2	1695	
Proposed	Modem MIB—Using SMIv2	1696	
Proposed	RDMS MIB—Using SMIv2	1697	
Draft	RIP Version 2 MIB Extension	1724	
Proposed	AppleTalk MIB	1742	
Proposed	SNADLC SDLC MIB Using SMIv2	1747	
Draft	IEEE 802.5 Token Ring MIB	1748	
Proposed	802.5 SSR MIB Using SMIv2	1749	
Draft	Remote Network Monitoring MIB	1757	
Proposed	Printer MIB	1759	
Experimental	TCP/IPX Connection MIB Specification	1792	
Draft	OSPF Version 2 MIB	1850	
Draft	Protocol Operations for SNMPv2	1905	
Draft	Transport Mappings for SNMPv2	1906	
Draft	MIB for SNMPv2	1907	
Draft	Coexistence Between SNMPV1 and SNMPV2	1908	
Proposed	Mobile IP MIB Definition Using SMIv2	2006	

Table 7.2 *(Continued)*

STATUS	NAME	RFC	STD
Proposed	IEEE 802.12 Interface MIB	2020	
Proposed	RMON MIB Using SMIv2	2021	
Proposed	DLSw MIB Using SMIv2	2024	
Proposed	Entity MIB Using SMIv2	2037	
Proposed	SNANAU APPC MIB Using SMIv2	2051	
Experimental	Traffic Flow Measurement Meter MIB	2064	
Proposed	Remote Network Monitoring MIB	2074	
Proposed	IP Forwarding Table MIB	2096	
Proposed	802.3 Repeater MIB Using SMIv2	2108	
Draft	Management Information Base for Frame	2115	
Proposed	ISDN MIB Using SMIv2	2127	
Proposed	Dial Control MIB using SMIv2	2128	
Proposed	Definitions of Managed Objects for APPN	2155	
Proposed	RSVP Management Information Base	2206	
Proposed	Integrated Services MIB Using SMIv2	2213	
Proposed	Integrated Services MIB Guar Serv Ext	2214	
Proposed	Interfaces Group MIB	2233	
Proposed	Definitions of Managed Objects for HPR	2238	
Proposed	IEEE 802.3 Medium Attachment Units MIB	2239	
Proposed	Network Services Monitoring MIB	2248	
Proposed	Mail Monitoring MIB	2249	
Proposed	IEEE 802.12 Repeater MIB	2266	
Proposed	Classical IP and ARP Over ATM MIB	2320	
Proposed	Ethernet-like Interface Types MIB	2358	
Proposed	Multicast/UNI 3.0/3.1 Based ATM MIB	2417	
Proposed	TCP MIB for IPv6	2452	
Proposed	UDP MIB for IPv6	2454	
Proposed	APPN MIB	2455	

Continues

Table 7.2   MIB Documents *(Continued)*

STATUS	NAME	RFC	STD
Proposed	APPN TRAPS MIB	2456	
Proposed	Extended Border Node MIB	2457	
Proposed	Textual Conventions, General Group MIB	2465	
Proposed	ICMPv6 Group MIB	2466	
Proposed	DSO MIB/DSOBUNDLE MIB	2494	
Proposed	DS1/E1/DS2/E2 MIB	2495	
Proposed	DS3/E3 Interface Type MIB	2496	
Proposed	Connection-Oriented Accounting MIB	2513	
Proposed	MIB for ATM Management	2515	
Proposed	SONET/SDH Interface Type MIB	2558	
Proposed	TN3270E Using SMIv2 MIB	2561	
Proposed	TN3270E-RT-MIB	2562	
Proposed	Application Management MIB	2564	
Proposed	APPN/HPR in IP Networks MIB	2584	

Simple Network Management Protocol

The Simple Network Management Protocol (SNMP) actually is quite simple: With IP, it uses a connectionless transport protocol (User Datagram Protocol) that carries data (both requests and replies) in simple message units. The complicated part of the SNMP is the infrastructure: the SMI and MIB structures that all compliant devices and systems must support. Within that infrastructure, which is really just a temple for where to store data and what to call it, SNMP operates by sending out a few basic messages.

Two types of entities are defined under SNMP: the agent that sits on every device or system that supports SNMP, and the manager, which can send and receive messages to and from agents for the purpose of collecting information about the state of the device and the network in general. There are two basic types of protocol interaction between agents and managers: a request/response interaction, where the manager asks for some information from the agent and the agent replies with the requested information, and the trap, which is sent out unilaterally by an agent when something untoward occurs that the manager might want to know about.

ATM-Related MIBs

As we see in more detail in Chapter 14, ATM requires several different MIBs, depending on the different ways in which it is used in conjunction with IP. Table 7.3 lists the four current MIB specifications for ATM. ATM must also conform with RFC 2233, "The Interfaces Group MIB Using SMIv2."

Table 7.3 RFCs Defining ATM-Related MIBs

RFC	TITLE
RFC 1695	Definitions of Managed Objects for ATM Management Version 8.0 Using SMIv2
RFC 2320	Definitions of Managed Objects for Classical IP and ARP Over ATM Using SMIv2 (IPOA-MIB)
RFC 2417	Definitions of Managed Objects for Multicast over UNI 3.0/3.1 Based ATM Networks
RFC 2515	Definitions of Managed Objects for ATM Management

Reading List

The reader is urged to check out the original RFCs for more information about SNMP, SMI, and MIB. Table 7.4 contains a selection of some documents in this area (other related documents are included in Tables 7.1, 7.2, and 7.3). Marshall Rose, long a key contributor to the ongoing SNMP effort, has written a book that provides an introduction to SNMP and related specifications titled *The Simple Book 2nd edition* (Prentice Hall, 1996).

Table 7.4 Network Management RFCs

RFC	TITLE
RFC 1155	Structure of Management Information
RFC 1212	Concise MIB Definitions

Continues

Table 7.4   Network Management RFCs *(Continued)*

RFC	TITLE
RFC 1229	Extensions to the Generic-Interface MIB
RFC 1441	Introduction to SNMPv2
RFC 1448	Protocol Operations for SNMPv2
RFC 2570	Introduction to Version 3 of the Internet-standard Network Management Framework
RFC 2572	Message Processing and Dispatching for the Simple Network Management Protocol (SNMP)
RFC 2578	Structure of Management Information Version 2 (SMIv2)

PART
Two

ATM Standards

Virtually all of the actual standards that define ATM are created outside the IETF. The ATM Forum handles development of the basic ATM technology. However, many standards and specifications are developed within the IETF that rely on, use, or interact with ATM. The rest of this book discusses these specifications.

Chapter 8, "Asynchronous Transfer Mode," starts out with an introduction to ATM itself, while Chapter 9, "IP over ATM," introduces some of the issues raised by attempting to use IP over ATM. Chapters 10, "Mapping IP onto ATM," and 11, "The ATM Forum Solutions," outline how the IETF and the ATM Forum, respectively, have approached the problem of mapping IP onto ATM. Chapter 12, "IP Routing through ATM," gets into the details of IP routing through ATM networks, while Chapter 13, "Managing Network Traffic," looks at the issues of managing network traffic, which means understanding how network resources can be reserved and quality of service assured in ATM and IP networks. Chapter 14, "ATM Management," returns to the issues raised in Chapter 7, "Network Management Fundamentals," and details some of the specifications for managing ATM networks using the Simple Network Management Protocol (SNMP) and the Structure of Management

Information (SMI). Finally, Chapter 15, "The Future of ATM and IP," provides an overview to the immediate future of ATM and IP, first by looking at how IPv6 will be run over ATM and then with brief summaries of IETF working group activities.

Asynchronous Transfer Mode

Asynchronous Transfer Mode (ATM) is not a single protocol that can coexist with IP, interoperating below IP on the protocol stack, but rather a complex networking technology in its own right. The ATM Forum identifies more than 60 different specifications necessary to define an ATM infrastructure. In this chapter, we provide an overview to ATM, how it works, and where its standards come from.

ATM Overview

ATM started out being called Broadband Integrated Services Digital Network (B-ISDN). The idea was to design a data communication technology that could carry any kind of data—voice, video, or computer data—across any kind—local or wide area—of network. The resulting technologies became known as ATM.

To grossly oversimplify, ATM nodes take upper-layer protocol data units (PDUs) and break them up into small, uniformly sized cells. Once the ATM node determines where the PDUs are bound, it sends them out along a virtual circuit (VC) connecting the source node with the destination. ATM circuits are created through ATM switches, with the nodes doing something called signaling to determine what path the cells should take across the ATM network cloud.

Figure 8.1 shows the simplified version of the ATM network. Inside that cloud can be almost any combination of ATM switches and other networks. In the simplest case, the only thing inside the cloud is a single ATM switch that is directly wired to both the source node and the destination node. The process of building a virtual circuit connecting the two nodes is relatively simple.

As we see later in the sections on ATM switching and virtual circuits, that cloud could contain a much more complicated picture. Perhaps the source node is connected to an ATM switch buried within an organizational network, as is the destination node. Creating a virtual circuit between the two nodes could require traversing several ATM switches in each network and then going across a public ATM network that links the organizations.

Figure 8.1 looks suspiciously like an IP network, if only in its use of a network cloud and a line linking two nodes through the cloud. ATM shares some important features with IP: They both use a hierarchical network structure, and both use devices inside the network cloud to get data from one node to another. However, as we see later in this chapter (and later in the book) when we talk about ATM switching and compare it to routing, there are important differences. While the links between nodes and through an IP network cloud generally represent the path that individual packets may take, the links between nodes and through an ATM network cloud represent the path that cells take through virtual

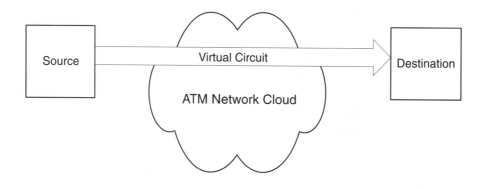

Figure 8.1   A very simple-minded view of an ATM network.

circuits. Whereas an IP network has some intelligence built in, so that it explicitly routes each packet, an ATM network depends on the end-points to negotiate the virtual circuits over which cells travel.

So far, we've introduced several terms that may be unfamiliar. They are explained later in this chapter. One thing that remains unexplained is why ATM is "asynchronous." Another is why ATM breaks PDUs up into 53-byte cells. To answer the last question first, ATM uses small cells rather than larger cells or variable length units to optimize performance. The small uniform size makes it possible to build hardware that can process cells entirely in registers rather than having to read in more data from buffers and then processing it through software (as IP routers have traditionally worked).

ATM was designed to perform well in all network environments from LANs to WANs. Performance is defined not just in terms of high-bandwidth transmission, but also in terms of low latency, guaranteed delivery, and low cost. How can all of these factors be maximized at once? They can't. But they shouldn't have to be: Sometimes data must get through, as with real-time audio transmissions where it is unacceptable to receive data discontinuously. Voice transmissions must be delivered at a uniform rate. Sending all the data from the previous five seconds does not help heal a five-second break in the transmission. On the other hand, a server synchronizing with another server overnight does not care if its data is received smoothly, as long as it is all delivered before the start of business the next morning. A lower rate can be negotiated with the understanding that higher-priority traffic (like a voice transmission) may displace the data delivery bits.

ATM provides a mechanism for specifying not only a virtual circuit between nodes but also a quality of service (QoS) level to be applied to the cells carrying data along that circuit. In order to achieve quality of service, some cells are flagged as "more urgent" while others are flagged as "less urgent." When a more urgent cell is received at a particular switch, that switch can determine that it has priority for switch resources at that moment and interrupt any other transmissions the switch was making. The switch stops transmitting cells with a lower priority for as long as it takes to get the higher-priority cells through. This explains why ATM is asynchronous: A switch can send as many or as few cells as it needs to, subject to its own resource limitations (and to any bandwidth reservations currently in effect—we'll discuss resource reservations in Chapter 13, "Managing Network Traffic").

Not only does this explain why ATM is asynchronous, but it also helps us understand why ATM cells are so small. After all, ATM cells carry a relatively high overhead, with 5 bytes of header to every 48 bytes of payload, which we discuss at greater length later in this chapter. Why not increase the size of the cell?

With a larger cell, a high-priority cell frequently arrives at an intermediate switch in the network just after that switch starts sending a lower-priority cell. If large cells were permitted, that high-priority cell would find itself cooling its heels waiting for the other cell to clear the switch before going off on its way. With small cells, waiting time is minimized, thus providing one more reason for the 53-byte ATM cell.

In the rest of this section, we briefly cover the basics of ATM.

ATM Reference Model

If ATM were simply a protocol defining a mechanism for interacting between nodes on a network, we would just call it a Layer 2 protocol and point to the OSI reference model to show how it fits in with IP and other protocols. However, ATM is not a single protocol, nor is it simple: It is a complex networking technology, and it has its own reference model. Figure 8.2 shows the B-ISDN reference model that underlies

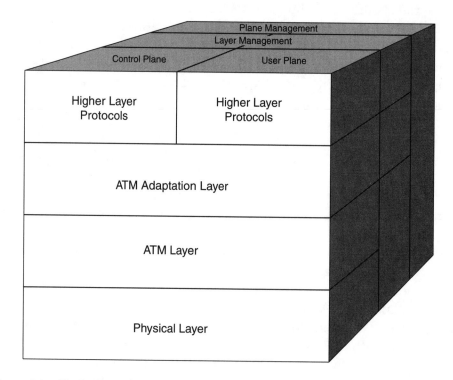

Figure 8.2   The B-ISDN reference model.

ATM. Unlike the OSI seven-layer reference model and the IP four-layer reference model, both of which are just one-dimensional layered protocol stacks, ATM's reference model has two dimensions: layers and planes.

First, the more familiar layers. At the very bottom is the physical layer, where bits are encoded onto a wire, fiber, or other medium over which they can be transmitted. The physical layer is divided into two sublayers in the ATM model: the lower sublayer, Physical Media Dependent (PMD), and the upper sublayer, Transmission Convergence (TC). The PMD sublayer handles the actual formatting, transmission, and receipt of bits on the fiber or wire. The TC sublayer acts as the interface between the PMD sublayer and the upper layers, accepting data in a standard format from the upper layers and framing it appropriately for the underlying network medium. ATM works over a wide variety of different network technologies, so the physical layer can be almost anything, and supported media includes SONET, xDSL, FDDI, Fiber Channel, and even Ethernet.

The ATM layer handles the ATM cells. This is where cells are formatted and relayed from one node to another and where cell destinations and paths are determined. Cell headers are inserted at this layer, and cells are handed down to the physical layer. Likewise, cells are received from the network at this layer, and cell headers are parsed for further processing. We get into the details of the ATM cell in the next section.

The next layer, the ATM Adaptation Layer (AAL), is where much of the action is with ATM. The AAL has two sublayers, but they work together to accept data from higher layers and turn that data into ATM cells. The lower sublayer, called the Segmentation and Reassembly (SAR) sublayer, rips outbound protocol data units into ATM cells for transmission and reconstitutes inbound protocol data units from ATM cells being received. The top sublayer, called the Convergence Sublayer (CS), serves as a place where data from more than one higher-level application can converge into the ATM stream and be passed down the stack to be processed and transmitted.

In some cases, the Convergence Sublayer is divided into two sub-sublayers, the Common Part CS (CPCS) and the Service-Specific CS (SSCS). The CPCS performs functions that are necessary for any type of network data, such as error correction and packet framing. The SSCS acts as an interface for any type of network application to be streamed into ATM, whether it is connection oriented or connectionless.

There are four different AALs defined for ATM, and each different one produces cells with a different format. We discuss AALs in a bit more detail later in this chapter.

Above the AAL are the "higher layers" of the model, which simply refer to whatever applications are generating the data to be transmitted across the ATM network. These higher layers can include TCP/IP, UDP/IP, and whatever other applications run on top of them or in parallel with them.

This takes care of the protocol stack part of the ATM model, but we are left with the concept of planes. At the front of the model are two planes: the Control Plane and the User Plane. The User Plane incorporates the part of the protocol stack that is most familiar—the movement of data up and down the stack to and from applications. The Control Plane handles signaling and the creation, release, and control of connections.

Behind the User and Control Planes lies the Management Plane. Some representations of the B-ISDN reference model split the Management Plane in two, with the part closer to the front of the diagram representing layer management and the part at the rear of the diagram representing plane management. The general idea is that behind the regular protocol layers lies a plane responsible for coordinating and managing all the different interactions between layers as well as between planes.

Ultimately, the B-ISDN reference model is no more a strict representation of reality than the OSI or IP references models. They are all simply models, useful for understanding ATM's functions and mechanisms and how they relate to each other.

In the next section, we take a closer look at the basic unit of exchange in ATM, the cell.

Protocol Data Units and Cells

The basic unit of exchange between ATM stations is the cell: a 53-byte unit, containing 5 bytes of header and 48 bytes of payload. This statement is overly simplistic and perhaps misleading, but it is useful as a starting point for discussion. Figure 8.3 shows a generic ATM cell: It is represented as a stack of 53 bytes, 8 bits wide. As we discover later in this chapter, some ATM cells have a slightly different header structure than others, but all conform to this generic format.

However, the cell is not ATM's basic protocol data unit (PDU). Rather, ATM accepts data in chunks and formats them in a much larger PDU, which is then sliced up into cells. The PDU is like an entire salami with its own protocol information incorporated. ATM slices up the salami very thinly and sends each slice out individually. When the slices arrive at their destination, they are reconstituted into a whole salami. Any

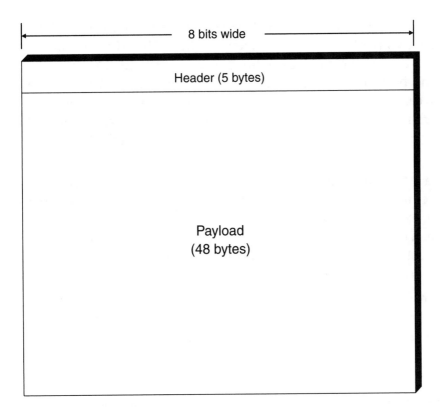

Figure 8.3   A generic ATM cell.

given cell contains only a small bit of data (no more than 48 bytes) and may contain none of the original PDU protocol header information. The upper layer protocol information is not accessible until the cells arrive at their destination and are put back together into the original PDU.

The cells contain header information that relates only to delivery within the ATM network. Five bytes is not a lot of room for header information. Figure 8.4 shows the actual headers of a typical ATM cell. Unlike in IP, where header fields conform to a 32-bit word length and never overlap word boundaries, several of the ATM cell header fields cross over byte boundaries.

ATM header fields include the following:

Generic Flow Control (GFC). This four-bit value is used locally only, meaning that it may be reset by a switch. It is sometimes used by vendors to carry proprietary information. In some cases, this field is absent (see the NNI/UNI section).

Virtual Path Identifier (VPI)/Virtual Channel Identifier (VCI).
These two fields are usually taken together. The VPI is defined as
an 8-bit field, and the VCI defined as a 16-bit field. Together, they
define how the cell is to be routed within an ATM switch and
between ATM switches. The VCI identifies a virtual channel (VC),
which is a circuit from one end device to another, through an ATM
switched network. The VPI identifies a virtual path (VP), which
carries groups of VCs between ATM switches.

Payload Type Indicator (PTI). This is a three-bit field that indicates
something about the cell contents. If the first bit is 0, then the payload contains user data; if 1, it contains management or control
data. The second bit indicates whether the cell has encountered
congestion (1) or not (0). The third bit signals the end of an AAL5
protocol data unit.

Cell Loss Priority (CLP). This single-bit flag indicates whether the
cell should be delivered even if it encounters congestion in the network. Applications that depend on the network to deliver all of the

← 8 bits wide →	
Generic Flow Control (GFC)	Virtual Path Identifier (VPI)
Virtual Path Identifier (VPI)	Virtual Channel Identifier (VCI)
Virtual Channel Identifier (VCI)	
Virtual Channel Identifier (VCI)	Payload Type (PTI) / Cell Loss Priority (CPI)
Header Error Control (HEC)	
Payload	

Figure 8.4   ATM cell headers.

bits, such as most traditional TCP/IP applications, set this bit to 0 to indicate a preference that the cell not be discarded. Applications that require a steady flow of data, such as video or audio, can't use bits that arrive too late, and so set this bit to 1 to indicate that late cells be discarded rather than delivered late.

Header Error Check (HEC). This eight-bit field contains a cyclic redundancy check (CRC) value for the first four bytes of the ATM cell header. When a switch calculates the CRC and it does not coincide with the HEC, the cell is usually discarded.

The ATM cell itself carries only enough information to get the cell from its source to its destination; higher-layer protocol information is stored within the PDU. However, the ATM Adaptation Layer is used to map data from the PDU into the cell.

ATM Adaptation Layers

We've already discussed the ATM cell and mentioned that it contains a slice of a PDU from a higher-layer application. There are different ways to slice and package the PDU, and these correspond to the ATM Adaptation Layer. There are four defined types of AAL, of which the most important for IP networking is AAL5 (others include AAL1, AAL2, and AAL3/4). The job of the AAL is to define how to map a PDU into a sequence of ATM cells. For example, AAL1 defines a mechanism by which the PDU is broken up into 47-byte chunks and packaged inside the ATM cell payload with a 1-byte prefix containing a sequence number and a CRC on the sequence number.

In contrast, AAL3/4 uses a relatively complex format for its PDU, which incorporates a 4-byte header and 4-byte trailer and padding to make sure that the PDU payload is aligned on a 4-octet boundary. This processing is done to the packet that AAL3/4 receives from up the protocol stack. Then, the PDU can be sliced up into cells, with each cell consisting of a 44-byte payload section with two bytes of header and two of trailer within the cell. The result is a relatively cumbersome approach to ATM.

In AAL5, which is the AAL most often used for carrying IP, the packet received from upper layers is turned into an ATM PDU by first padding it out so it fits evenly into a number of ATM cells and an 8-byte trailer is calculated and added to the PDU. The AAL5 PDU trailer consists of two 1-byte fields—User-to-User (UU) and Common Part Indicator (CPI)—

neither of which is used in most cases, followed by a 2-byte length field and a 4-byte CRC field, both of which are used.

The AAL5 PDU consists of $(48n + x + y + 8)$ bytes, where x is the number of bytes in the original packet in excess of a number evenly divisible by 48, and y is the number of pad bytes, such that $(x + y + 8) = 48$. The PDU can be any size up to 65,535 bytes long. Once the AAL5 PDU is created, it can be cut into ATM cells simply by dividing it up into 48-byte payloads and loading them into cells.

AAL5 was originally designed by IBM and has become a standard for ATM data transmission because of its simplicity and efficiency. Rather than wasting any of the cell payload on adaptation layer headers or trailers, the AAL5 packages a full complement of 48 bits of real PDU payload into the payload section of every cell except for the last cell, which contains a trailer and padding, if necessary.

Virtual Paths and Virtual Circuits

Looking at the ATM cell headers raises several questions, including what's the deal with virtual paths and virtual channels? To make it simple, look at Figure 8.5. The virtual channel (or virtual circuit, or VC) itself links two end nodes. It is possible there might be more than one virtual channel between those two nodes (for example, one channel could use lower-cost switches and another channel might use higher-cost switches), but only those two nodes are connected by a virtual

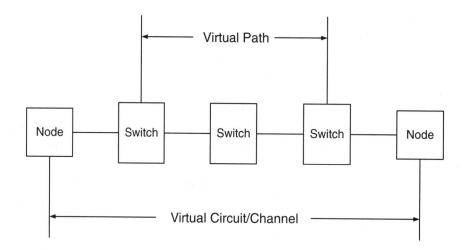

Figure 8.5 Virtual paths and virtual channels.

channel. However, the switches that handle the data being transmitted across a virtual channel don't really care who the endpoints are, just the endpoint switches. There may be hundreds of other nodes that connect to each of the endpoint ATM switches, with a staggering number of potential VCs linking each of the hundreds of nodes on one switch to each of the hundreds of nodes on the other switch. Since the end nodes are relevant only to themselves and to the switch they are connected to, the concept of a virtual path is used to aggregate all the possible virtual channels that might be carried between one switch and another.

A virtual circuit is defined by the path from one device on an ATM network and another device on an ATM network, traveling through at least one switch. Without the switch or switches in the middle, it's not a virtual channel, it's a real channel. The switched network in the middle makes it virtual. A VC is identified by a virtual channel identifier (VCI), which is a value that represents the VC path.

Two different types of VC are encountered in the world of ATM: the permanent VC (PVC) and the switched VC (SVC). PVCs are used mostly in smaller ATM networks and often in the earlier stages of ATM deployment. PVCs are created by hand, so that a channel from one node to another is configured statically in the network. This approach simplifies the process of making connections because there is no need for signaling between stations. However, it also complicates matters by requiring a manual process for each pair of stations that are to be linked. PVCs also become unwieldy as the network grows in size, as the number of possible circuits between nodes increases. Switches must allocate memory resources to hold path information for PVCs. In large networks, the number of PVCs stored in memory can easily overwhelm the switch.

As implementers deploy ATM in larger networks and gain experience with growing ATM networks, the switched VC becomes more important. An ATM station sending data to a remote station builds an SVC dynamically through the switched ATM network, and the SVC is torn down after the communication is complete.

Keeping in mind ATM's provenance as a telecommunications technology, the difference between PVCs and SVCs can be viewed as the difference between maintaining a database of circuit information to link every telephone subscriber in the country and building up a circuit on the fly whenever someone wants to make a call. We examine how ATM data is switched and how stations create circuits in the next section.

NNI AND UNI

In ATM, there is a difference between the connection between two network clouds and the connection between a user station and a network. An ATM edge device—a computer or other device connecting to an ATM network as a user node—connects to an ATM network (switch) through a User-Network Interface (UNI). Several different UNIs are defined; the ones most commonly referenced in Internet standards include UNI 3.0, 3.1, and 4.0. ATM node addresses vary depending on the network interface definition.

ATM switches, each of which is effectively its own network, are linked through the Network-Network Interface (NNI). The difference is important inasmuch as cell headers for NNI paths may be slightly different than headers for UNI paths.

ATM Addressing

IPv4 may run out of address space soon, but the ATM address space is probably safe for awhile. Each ATM station has a 20-byte address, which is globally unique within the domain. In other words, no two stations may have the same address in a global ATM network, though two nodes in two distinct ATM networks that have no point of connectivity could have the same address.

At 160 bits, the ATM address space can support (in theory) as many as $(2^{160} - 1)$ different nodes. This is a very, very large number.

The ATM Forum specification breaks the 20-byte ATM End System Address (AESA) into two separate parts. The most significant bits of the address define the Initial Domain Part (IDP), while the rest of the address is called the Domain Specific Part (DSP). Each of these parts contains other parts. Figure 8.6 shows how this works. Missing from this figure are the relative sizes of the IDP and DSP. This is intentional: The precise contents of the ATM address vary depending on the address format in use.

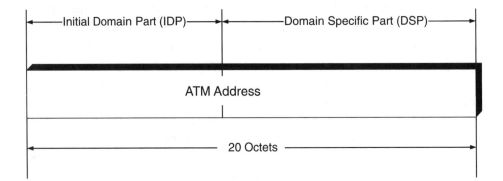

Figure 8.6 A generalized view of the ATM address.

Every ATM address contains an Address Format Identifier (AFI) in the first octet. This is followed by an Initial Domain Identifier (IDI). The length of the IDI depends on the ATM address format in use, but in any case it (along with the AFI) identifies the high-level domain in which that address exists.

The Domain Specific Part (DSP) of the address uniquely identifies the ATM station within the domain (as defined in the IDP). It contains a High Order DSP (HO-DSP), which acts as a further hierarchical identifier within the initial domain, and a low-order part that contains two more pieces: a 6-byte End-System Identifier (ESI) and a one-byte Selector (SEL). The ESI can be a hardware address for the end system, similar to the 48-bit Ethernet address. The Selector octet is used only by end stations for multiplexing: Different inbound data streams can be addressed to the same end station but to different SEL values.

Three formats were defined by the ATM Forum in 1993, when it specified UNI 3.0: the E.164 NSAP encapsulated, the Data Country Code (DCC), and the International Code Designator (ICD) formats. Figure 8.7 shows these three common ATM address formats. The E.164 standard is

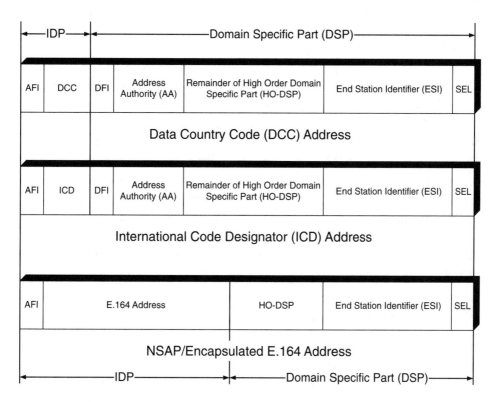

Figure 8.7 Three ATM address formats.

defined for Frame Relay and ISDN and is intended to be used to connect an end system with an E.164 numbered network. The embedded E.164 format is often referred to as an NSAP (Network Service Access Point) format and is very similar, but is not a true NSAP address.

The DCC and ICD addresses are pretty much the same except for the contents of the second two octets of the address, and even there the second address field contains pretty much the same information: a country or organization code. For DCC addresses, the second field is labeled Data Country Code (DCC) and contains a two-byte ISO country code. For ICD addresses, the second field is labeled the International Code Designator (ICD) and contains a two-byte code identifying an international organization (the codes are assigned by the British Standards Institution).

Following the ICD/DCC field is the Domain Format Identifier (DFI), which identifies the format being used for the rest of the high-order part of the address. The Address Authority (AA) is usually a three-byte field containing an organizational ID. From there, organizing the rest of the high-order DSP is up to the organization referred to in the AA: They can use that six bytes for building their own hierarchical structure based on physical layout, departments, or switches.

We've gone on in depth about the ATM address space so that the reader can make connections with the way the IP address space works. Both are hierarchical, and both provide a certain degree of latitude for network organization to the local domains. Understanding ATM addresses makes it a bit easier to understand how ATM signaling is accomplished, which in turn makes it a bit easier to understand ATM as a technology. So far, we've covered the ATM reference model, ATM cells and protocol data units, virtual paths and circuits, but it may not yet be clear how one end station can create a virtual circuit to another end station if the network itself has no intelligence (as is the case in an IP routed network) and if the end stations themselves have no prior knowledge of each other's existence. This mystery is cleared up in the next section.

ATM Switching and Signaling

We've talked about ATM switches, switching, and signaling throughout this chapter without really defining them. We've also noted that ATM networks depend on switching while IP networks depend on routing (usually), which is an important distinction.

Switching

Much of what we've introduced in this chapter doesn't truly make sense until ATM switching is understood, so here it is in a nutshell.

An ATM switch is a relatively simple device, as graphically shown in Figure 8.8. It has ports for inbound data, ports for outbound data, a switching fabric, and a switching table. The switching fabric or mesh allows the switch to do its thing with cells, which is send a cell coming in on an inbound port out of an appropriate outbound port. The switching table is a facility for mapping virtual circuit identifiers onto inbound and outbound ports, so that the switch can keep track of which outbound port to send cells with a particular VCI coming in on a particular inbound port.

A switch behaves like a freight terminus for data. The ATM cells are like shipping containers, with a destination VC identifier (VCI) stenciled on the side (in the cell header). When a cell comes in, the switch looks at the VCI on the cell and then compares it to its switching table. When it finds a match, the switch rewrites the cell, giving it a new VCI

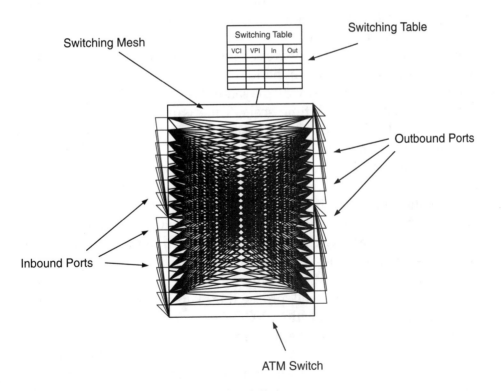

Figure 8.8   A functional depiction of an ATM switch.

that works when it arrives at the next switch. Unlike in IP, the VCI (and VPI) are rewritten with each switch hop.

The switch keeps track of where to send a cell that it receives on any given inbound interface, based on what the VCI/VPI values are. When it forwards the cells, the switch rewrites the header values so that the next hop switch can figure out what to do with those cells. We've mentioned before that ATM relies on the endpoints of the links to negotiate its connections, and so far we've been talking about switches as if they somehow know where everything is supposed to go. The next section introduces the concept of ATM signaling, the mechanism by which the endpoints manage to create a virtual circuit.

Signaling

Before an end station can create a switched VC, it must know its own ATM address as well as the ATM address of the destination station. This is equivalent to knowing the telephone number of someone you are trying to call. Knowing these addresses, the originating station can submit a signal request to its immediate network connection, the switch. As we see in Chapter 10, "Mapping IP onto ATM," getting the ATM address of the destination station is not a trivial matter when using IP as the network layer protocol. For now, we can just assume that the calling station has the destination address in hand.

The process is graphically displayed in Figure 8.9. This figure shows system interactions on a time scale. Time is moving forward as you move down the diagram. The first step is a SETUP message sent from the source to the switch. This message specifies the ATM addresses of both endpoint systems. Other items sent in this message include AAL parameters, traffic parameters, QoS parameters, and other data necessary for the signaling protocol being used (signaling protocols can be quite complex and are beyond the scope of this text). When the switch receives this message, two things happen: First, it figures out what to do with the signaling request and sends its own SETUP message off; then, it sends a CALL PROCEEDING message back to the originating node that indicates the call is, well, proceeding. This message also contains a VPI/VCI for the VC connection (VCC) being set up.

An ATM switch is a good approximation of an ATM network, and it is possible to represent the ATM network as a cloud while explaining whether the source and destination are separated by a single ATM switch or an entire public network. The reason is simple: Every edge

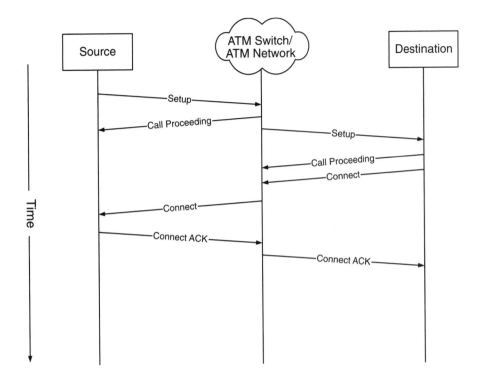

Figure 8.9 ATM signaling.

device is connected to a switch, and no edge device has any direct inter-action with any other devices except through the mediation of that switch. What's on the other side is irrelevant, at least from the point of view of the edge device. When the source edge device begins signaling with the SETUP message, it relies completely on the switch to which it is directly connected to act on its behalf in setting up the rest of the circuit.

The switch uses the source and destination ATM address informa-tion, along with its own knowledge of the network topology, to figure out where the next SETUP message should go. The process continues on through the ATM network until the called party is reached. At that point, the destination station sends off the same CALL PROCEEDING message that all the other stations sent, but shortly after—once it real-izes that the signaling is intended to initiate a VC with itself and decides that it wants to accept that circuit—it sends off a CONNECT message indicating that the VCC can be initiated. The CONNECT mes-sage propagates back down the line to the originating system, at which point an acknowledgment (ACK) of the CONNECT is sent back through the network. When the ACK is received at the destination, the circuit is complete and the call can proceed.

As each of these steps is taken through the ATM network, the intervening switches build up the circuit by keeping track of the VCI/VPIs associated with the new VC as well as what the VC links. When the VC is broken down, the caller sends a RELEASE message to its neighboring switch. Rather than wait until that RELEASE message propagates to the end of the VC, the local switch passes the RELEASE message on to the next switch in the VC and immediately after that sends a RELEASE COMPLETE message back to the source station. This makes VC releases much quicker than building the VC.

How do the switches know enough about the network to be able to make these decisions? One way is to use the Private Network-to-Network Interface (PNNI) specification. PNNI details various mechanisms that allow switches to exchange information with each other about connectivity status as well as for making sure that bandwidth is available and that quality of service agreements can be accomplished. Network management tasks can also be carried out through PNNI.

ATM Quality of Service (QoS)

On an Ethernet network, service is on a first-come, first-served basis. When a system wants to send some data, it checks to see whether anyone else is sending and waits until the wire is clear. If two systems try to send at the same time and their data collides, they both back off and wait to resend, using an algorithm that prevents a recollision. Each time a node needs to send a frame, it goes through the same process. If the network is very busy then, it may take a while to get that data sent.

Most popular Internet applications are not terribly sensitive to network delays, and some are quite forgiving. However, that may be because any applications that *are* sensitive to such delays tend not to work very well on the Internet. A file transfer may be delayed as it goes through, but it is eventually completed. However, many applications that would be nice to run over the Internet or other IP networks don't work well because of delivery delays. Voice over IP (VoIP) is one example, as is almost any real-time application.

There are two issues that would be nice to solve. The first is how to assign different values to chunks of data such that some chunks can get special (or at least, different from default) treatment. The second is how to notify the network that an application needs some guaranteed amount of bandwidth. The first problem is usually referred to as quality

> ### NBMA NETWORKS
>
> ATM is a nonbroadcast multiple access (NBMA) network and so is X.25, Frame Relay, and others. The key characteristic of an NBMA network is that it does not have a mechanism by which a single transmission can be picked up by more than one node (multicast). By way of contrast, on traditional Ethernets, all nodes are attached to the same wire and all nodes' network interfaces pick up all the transmissions on that wire. When a unicast is sent, all stations (except for the intended recipient) detect the unicast's destination address, determine it is not for them, and ignore it. When a broadcast or multicast is sent out, all stations detect the multicast or broadcast address and process the transmission (if they want to). NBMA networks, on the other hand, use a network device to repeat broadcasts and multicasts, sending a separate copy of the message to each recipient.

of service; the second is termed resource reservation. These problems aren't easy to solve in a broadcast network, that is, a network where all nodes have equal access to the network medium, where any node can send data over the network at any given time, and where all nodes have access to all transmissions. However, quality of service and resource reservation are a lot easier in nonbroadcast multiple access (NBMA) networks (see "NBMA Networks") where all transmissions are mediated through a central network cloud (or switch).

When a circuit is set up, the initiating station can specify that the data being sent is part of a data flow, for example, a video feed or a terminal emulation session. There are different requirements for handling that data depending on the application that generates the data. The video feed may require 1Mbps of bandwidth for the entire duration of the session; the terminal emulation session may have no performance requirements other than that no data should ever be thrown out even if the network is congested.

The requirement for 1Mbps of bandwidth may not be a problem for a network with a 155.52Mbps backplane, as many ATM networks have. However, the video feed must have 1Mbps throughout the transmission, not as an average. Sending 120Mbps for one second is not equivalent to sending 1Mbps for two minutes. When the circuit carrying that feed is set up, the source station can indicate its requirements for the circuit quality of service as part of the signaling process.

ATM Standards

ATM is a relatively new technology, especially used with the Internet Protocol. The ATM Forum, an international industry consortium with hundreds of members, was formed in 1991 with the mission of assisting the deployment of ATM through the creation of interoperable standards. An important part of the ATM Forum is the ATM Forum Technical Committee, which cooperates with international standards bodies on the selection of appropriate standards, resolution of differences among standards, and recommendations for new standards where none exist or where those that exist are inappropriate.

The ATM Forum sponsors some activities that are open to the public, but most are not. Membership in the forum is available in three tiers:

Principal Membership. Principal members may attend and participate in all ATM Forum meetings (committee meetings as well as annual membership meetings). They may vote on any forum issue, and they have access to any Forum documents or meeting minutes. The cost of the Principal membership is $14,000 per year.

Auditing Membership. Auditing members can attend and participate at the annual meeting and may have access to working documents and meeting minutes, but may not vote or attend committee meetings. Auditing membership costs $2,000 per year.

User Membership. User members can attend the annual meeting as well as User Committee meetings and may vote on issues raised in the User Committee or in working groups. They have access to all working documents and meeting minutes. User membership costs $1,500 per year.

ATM standards are developed by members of the ATM Forum Technical Committee. Only principal members may serve on this committee, so ATM Forum standards workgroups are far from open to individuals. Table 8.1 lists the specifications that were included in the ATM Forum's "Anchorage Accord," a 1996 meeting in Anchorage, Alaska, at which about 60 specifications were endorsed as part of a stable and interoperable platform for network implementations. Since then, additional specifications have been approved only a few at a time.

Though the ATM Forum technical working groups are private, ATM Forum specifications are available online by FTP from the ATM Forum Web site (see the Reading List section below) in various different formats including .rtf (Rich Text Format), Microsoft Word, PostScript, and .pdf (Adobe Acrobat).

Table 8.1   Specifications Included in the ATM Forum Anchorage Accord

BISDN Inter Carrier Interface Specification v2.0
Addendum to BISDN Inter Carrier Interface Specification v2.0
Data Exchange Interface v1.0
Integrated Local Management Interface Specification v4.0
LAN Emulation over ATM v1.0
LAN Emulation v1.0 Implementation Tip Sheet
LAN Emulation Client Management Specification v1.0
LAN Emulation over ATM v1.0 Addendum
LAN Emulation Servers Management Specification v1.0
Customer Network Management (CNM) for ATM Public Network Service (M3 Specification)
M4 Interface Requirements and Logical MIB
CMIP Specification for the M4 Interface
M4 Network View Interface Requirements and Logical MIB
M4 Network View Requirements and Logical MIB Addendum
Circuit Emulation Services Interworking Requirements Logical CMIP MIB
M4 Network View CMIP MIB Specification v1.0
AAL Management for the M4 "NE View" Interface
ATM Physical Medium Dependent Interface for 155Mb/s over Twisted Pair Cable
DS1 Physical Layer Specification
UTOPIA Specification, Level 1, v2.01
Mid-range Physical Layer Specification for Category 3 Unshielded Twisted-Pair
6,312Kbps UNI Specification v1.0
E3 Public UNI
UTOPIA Specification, Level 2, v1.0
Physical Interface Specification for 25.6 Mb/s Over Twisted Pair Cable
A Cell-Based Transmission Convergence Sublayer for Clear Channel Interfaces
622.08Mbps Physical Layer Specification
155.52Mb/s Physical Layer Specification for Category 3 Unshielded Twisted Pair

Continues

Table 8.1   Specifications Included in the ATM Forum Anchorage Accord *(Continued)*

Addendum to ATM Physical Medium Dependent Interface Specification for 155Mb/s over Twisted Pair Cable DS3
Physical Layer Interface Specification
155.52Mbps Physical Layer Interface Specification for Short Wavelength Lasers
Workable Interface Requirements Example
E1 Physical Layer Interface Specification
Interim Inter-Switch Signaling Protocol (IISP) Specification v1.0
Private Network-Network Interface Specification v1.0
Private Network-Network Interface Specification v1.0 Addendum (Soft PVC MIB)
Addendum to Private Network-Network Interface Specification v1.0 for ABR Parameter Negotiating
Frame Based User to Network Interface (FUNI) Specification
Circuit Emulation Service Interoperability Specification
Native ATM Services: Semantic Description v1.0
Audiovisual Multimedia Services: Video on Demand Specification v1.1
ATM Name System Specification v1.0
ATM User-Network Interface (UNI) Signaling Specification v4.0
Addendum to UNI Signaling 4.0 for ABR Parameter Negotiation
Introduction to ATM Forum Test Specifications v1.0
PICS Proforma for the DS3 Physical Layer Interface v1.0
PICS Proforma for the SONET STS-3c Physical Layer Interface v1.0
PICS Proforma for the 100Mbps Multimode Fibre Physical Layer Interface v1.0
PICS Proforma for the UNI 3.0 ATM Layer
Conformance Abstract Test Suite for the UNI 3.0 ATM Layer of Intermediate Systems
Interoperability Abstract Test Suite for the Physical Layer
PICS Proforma for the DS1 Physical Layer Interface
Conformance Abstract Test Suite for the UNI 3.0 ATM Layer of End Systems
PICS Proforma for AAL5 Type 5
PICS Proforma for the 51.84Mbps Mid-Range Physical Layer Interface
Conformance Abstract Test Suite for the UNI 3.1 ATM Layer of Intermediate Systems
PICS Proforma for the 25.6Mb/s over Twisted Pair Cable Physical Layer

Table 8.1 *(Continued)*

Conformance Abstract Test Suite for the ATM Adaptation Layer(AAL) Type 5 Common Part (Part 1)
PICS Proforma for UNI 3.1 ATM Layer
Conformance Abstract Test Suite for UNI 3.1 ATM Layer of End Systems
Conformance Abstract Test Suite for the SSCOP for UNI 3.1
PICS Proforma for the 155Mb/s over Twisted Cable Physical Medium Dependent Interface
Traffic Management Specification 4.0
Addendum to Traffic Management 4.0 for ABR Parameter Negotiation
User to Network Interface Specification v3.1

Reading List

The best resource for ATM Forum specifications is the ATM Forum itself. Table 8.2 lists some useful URLs for the ATM Forum and the ITU.

Table 8.2 Web Resources for ATM Standards

SITE DESCRIPTION	URL
The ATM Forum (home page)	www.atmforum.com/
ATM Forum Technical Specifications page	www.atmforum.com/atmforum/specs/specs.html
ATM Forum Approved Specifications page	www.atmforum.com/atmforum/specs/approved.html
ATM Forum FTP site	ftp://ftp.atmforum.com/pub/
ITU	www.itu.int/

IP over ATM

Using IP over ATM raises quite a few nontrivial problems. At a very basic level, there are questions of how to map an IP datagram into an ATM protocol data unit and how to do multicasts and broadcasts over a network that can easily be overwhelmed by them. Then, there are deeper questions about how to do internetworking. ATM provides a networking environment that can stand on its own, providing end-to-end data delivery—in some ways like the service provided by IP. Thus, trying to use it as a transport mechanism for IP can become complicated. In many other link layer protocols used to transport IP (like that provided by Ethernet), the link layer provides transport services across a well-delimited network or direct connection. A large ATM network can interconnect many other smaller ATM networks, just as the Internet interconnects many other smaller IP networks. How can ATM and IP be made to interact in a way that allows IP to use ATM quality of service features? How can higher-layer applications use both IP and ATM to reserve bandwidth resources?

In this chapter, we look at how IP and ATM interface and discuss why interoperation between the two is not always simple. Then, we look at some of the technical issues related to the implementation of IP over ATM, things like point-to-multipoint (multicast/broadcast) transmissions in ATM, managing the Address Resolution Protocol (ARP) and related issues specific for ATM, and the importance of the Next Hop Resolution Protocol (NHRP). Next, we discuss two approaches to deploying IP over ATM: Classic IP and ARP over ATM (IPOA) and LAN Emulation (LANE). We also discuss routing issues related to running IP and ATM, issues related to IP and ATM Quality of Service (QoS) considerations, and issues related to resource reservation. Finally, we also introduce Multiprotocol Label Switching (MPLS), one of the important specifications that will soon be incorporated into official IETF standards.

As we introduce the issues, we also introduce the RFCs that elaborate on these issues, and we return to these documents in later chapters.

IP over/through/on ATM: Issues

The world of IP includes everything that runs over IP (from application protocols like HTTP and email to transport protocols like TCP and UDP) and everything that IP runs on top of (mostly link layer protocols like Ethernet). ATM is not merely another link layer protocol over which IP can happily run although, as we see, it is often treated as such for simplicity sake. It can support very large, heterogeneous, interconnected networks linking many different types of devices and systems. It provides what amounts to services normally provided at layer 3 and even layer 4 in IP networks, such as quality of service and resource reservations (both defined at layer 3 in IP and related protocols).

By treating ATM as if it were simply a layer 2 transport, you lose access to a lot of the goodies built into ATM. You can't easily access its QoS features nor can you easily do resource reservation. However, it certainly simplifies the process of building an IP network that incorporates ATM networks.

The problem of using ATM features through IP networks crops up again and again throughout this book. It is one of the manifestations of the difficulty of doing ATM with IP, but it also demonstrates the potential that IP/ATM networking holds. Issues related to the integration of IP and ATM that we introduce in this chapter and discuss at greater length throughout the book include the following:

Encapsulating IP in ATM. Even if you treat ATM as a simple link layer protocol on a par with Ethernet, you've still got to define mechanisms for encapsulating IP in ATM. RFC 1483, "Multiprotocol Encapsulation over ATM Adaptation Layer 5," defines how this encapsulation is accomplished. Written in 1993, RFC 1483 is still current—for the moment. An update draft is currently in the works.

Address Resolution. Again, any link layer protocol must provide a mechanism by which nodes can figure out who they are and where to send data. The Address Resolution Protocol (ARP), as defined in RFC 826, "An Ethernet Address Resolution Protocol," is best suited to link layer protocols that can easily broadcast requests, such as Ethernet. Broadcasts under ATM are more complicated and not as easily accomplished as in Ethernet. Thus, a different approach is taken to create an ATMARP, as defined in RFC 2225, "Classical IP and ARP over ATM." We also look at Inverse ARP and how it works under ATM, as defined in RFC 2390, "Inverse Address Resolution Protocol."

Routing/next hop Resolution. With Classical IP Over ATM (IPOA), an ATM network is treated as a logical IP subnet. All of the functions performed within an IP subnet, including routing, are mapped directly onto the ATM network. This is not always practical, and often a single ATM network will support more than one IP subnet. In these cases, routing can be complicated: A packet might hit several routers, passing through several ATM switches, just to arrive at a destination that is within the ATM network. It would be nice to have a mechanism that allows the packet to bypass all those routers and switches to go directly to the next hop. The Next Hop Resolution Protocol (NHRP), defined in RFC 2332, "NBMA Next Hop Resolution Protocol (NHRP)," defines such a mechanism.

Resource Reservation. This is the mechanism by which applications can notify the network of their need for some amount of bandwidth over a certain period of time during which the network responds by making that bandwidth available (or by notifying the application that the resources are unavailable). The Resource Reservation Protocol is specified in RFC 2205, "Resource ReSerVation Protocol (RSVP)—Version 1 Functional Specification." It specifies a protocol that can be used to request specific qualities of service from the network, though this type of function is best served in ATM. Several RFCs, including RFC 2379, "RSVP over

ATM Implementation Guidelines," define how RSVP and ATM work together. RSVP and Quality of Service are inextricably linked.

Quality of Service (QoS). IP has had a Type of Service field in its header since 1981. This was originally intended to carry an "an indication of the abstract parameters of the quality of service desired," according to RFC 791, "Internet Protocol." This feature has largely been unused both because it is virtually impossible to implement in any meaningful way as defined and because link layer protocols such as Ethernet don't support QoS differentiation. At the network layer, you might indicate that a packet needs special treatment, but that treatment cannot be specified at the lower layers. ATM also has quality of service (QoS) features, designed to be coordinated with traffic flows so that QoS can be implemented in a meaningful way. Thus, there are two issues related to QoS, ATM, and IP: how to let IP routers take advantage of the QoS features of ATM and how to let IP applications take advantage of ATM QoS. RFC 2386, "A Framework for QoS-based Routing in the Internet," discusses QoS issues in a general way as does RFC 2212, "Specification of Guaranteed Quality of Service." RFC 2381, "Interoperation of Controlled-Load Service and Guaranteed Service with ATM," discusses some of the issues related to using ATM QoS features.

The rest of this chapter highlights some of these issues and provides some guidance to RFCs that relate to implementing IP and ATM in an Internet-standard environment.

IP over ATM

It would be great if IP could integrate simply on top of ATM networks in such a way as to provide maximum flexibility and maximum performance, but that is not the case. ATM is not a simple link layer protocol, but a powerful networking technology in its own right.

At the most basic level, when encapsulating a higher-layer protocol like IP in ATM, you must start with a standard for doing that encapsulation. RFC 1483, "Multiprotocol Encapsulation over ATM Adaptation Layer 5," defines how upper-layer protocols, including IP, can be encapsulated within the ATM Adaptation Layer 5. This encapsulation is fundamental for most IP/ATM activity, and this specification is cited by most RFCs covering ATM topics.

Three other fundamental areas must be attended to when mapping IP over ATM. First, there must be some mechanism for doing address resolution. The Address Resolution Protocol (ARP) defined in RFC 826 is specifically designed for use in Ethernets and other broadcast-enabled environments. ATM is a nonbroadcast environment and therefore requires that special mechanisms be defined to create an ATM ARP, such as is described in RFC 2225, "Classical IP and ARP over ATM." Inverse ARP is described in RFC 2390, "Inverse Address Resolution Protocol."

The other two functions, multicast and broadcast, are not included in the basic "classical" approach. They are, however, supported for IP over ATM through the use of special servers: The Multicast Address Resolution Server (MARS) acts on behalf of the attached nodes within its service area. The MARS approach can be adapted for use as a broadcast relay as well. MARS is described in RFC 2022, "Support for Multicast over UNI 3.0/3.1 based ATM Networks," and the mechanism for adapting the MARS concept for broadcast is described in RFC 2226, "IP Broadcast over ATM Networks."

The next generation of the Internet Protocol brings some twists for doing IPv6 over ATM, and these are described in RFC 2491, "IPv6 over Non-Broadcast Multiple Access (NBMA) Networks," and RFC 2492, "IPv6 over ATM Networks." Table 9.1 lists some of the RFCs that describe how IP works over ATM.

Table 9.1   IP over ATM RFCs

RFC	STATUS	TITLE
RFC 826	STD 37	Ethernet Address Resolution Protocol or Converting Network Protocol Addresses to 48 bit Ethernet Address for Transmission on Ethernet Hardware
RFC 1483	Proposed STD	Multiprotocol Encapsulation over ATM Adaptation Layer 5
RFC 1735	Experimental	NBMA Address Resolution Protocol (NARP)
RFC 1755	Proposed STD	ATM Signaling Support for IP over ATM
RFC 1932	Informational	IP over ATM: A Framework Document
RFC 2022	Proposed STD	Support for Multicast over UNI 3.0/3.1-based ATM Networks
RFC 2121	Informational	Issues affecting MARS Cluster Size
RFC 2149	Informational	Multicast Server Architectures for MARS-based ATM multicasting
RFC 2225	Proposed STD	Classical IP and ARP over ATM

Continues

Table 9.1   IP over ATM RFCs *(Continued)*

RFC	STATUS	TITLE
RFC 2226	Proposed STD	IP Broadcast over ATM Networks
RFC 2390	Draft STD	Inverse Address Resolution Protocol
RFC 2417	Proposed STD	Definitions of Managed Objects for Multicast over UNI 3.0/3.1 based ATM Networks
RFC 2443	Experimental	A Distributed MARS Service Using SCSP
RFC 2491	Proposed STD	IPv6 over Non-Broadcast Multiple Access (NBMA) Networks
RFC 2492	Proposed STD	IPv6 over ATM Networks

LAN Emulation

Classical IP over ATM works, but it does not take advantage of the richness of the ATM technology. There are other mechanisms defined for doing multiprotocol networking over ATM, but they are not sanctioned by the IETF—at least not yet. Another option is LAN Emulation (LANE), a product of the ATM Forum.

LAN Emulation (LANE) takes the approach used by Classical IP over ATM even further: The ATM network is treated like a layer 2 medium, and the LANE architecture specifies that nodes can be attached to an emulated LAN that behaves just like a real LAN. Assuming that the drivers are installed, any network protocol stack (IP, IPX, whatever) can access, through a standard interface like the Network Driver Interface Specification (NDIS) or Open Data-Link Interface (ODI), an ATM network in the same way that the same protocol stack can access an Ethernet/IEEE 802.3 network or token ring/IEEE 802.5 network.

With LANE, nodes can be organized into emulated LANs that span an ATM cloud and that behave just like their real LAN counterparts. An emulated LAN can be bridged with a real LAN and can be set to emulate either an Ethernet or a token ring LAN. LANE defines different entities that operate across ATM to make it behave like a LAN. These include the LAN emulation server, LAN emulation configuration server, the "broadcast and unknown server," and the LAN emulation client. We discuss these entities at greater length in Chapter 11, "The ATM Forum Solutions." LANE differs from IPOA in that IPOA works over raw ATM and uses ATM circuits directly to carry data, whereas LANE sits on top of ATM and makes it accessible to any protocol, including IP. In theory, using IP over LANE should be very simple; we'll see where the complications come up in Chapter 11.

LANE does not stand alone, but rather works in tandem with the ATM Forum standard for Multiprotocol Over ATM (MPOA). One of the problems with LANE is that it carves these nice little virtual LANs out of the ATM cloud and makes them behave as if they are real live LANs.

This is great for some things, especially for simplifying Ethernet or token ring to ATM migrations, but less great for taking advantage of the benefits of ATM. For example, if you've got an emulated LAN sitting in the middle of a great big ATM cloud, you've got to figure out how to route data to nodes on that emulated LAN. Under raw LANE, this means getting the data there through actual bridges or routing it through routers. However, this can also mean that data coming from a node on an ATM network might pass across one or more routers (all within the ATM cloud, or maybe even exiting the ATM cloud and re-entering it later) to make a trip that could much more easily be accomplished through a direct VC between the sender and recipient. MPOA works with LANE and with the Next Hop Resolution Protocol (NHRP), which is covered in Chapter 12, "IP Routing through ATM," to figure out short cuts in cases like the one we just described.

Though not IETF standards, LANE and MPOA are important aspects of ATM networking. The ATM Forum is responsible for developing these standards, and they are available at the ATM Forum Web site, www.atmforum.com/. Table 9.2 shows some of the important ATM Forum standards for LANE, MPOA, and related specifications.

Table 9.2   ATM Forum Specifications

DOCUMENT TITLE	URL
LAN Emulation over ATM Version 2	ftp://ftp.atmforum.com/pub/approved-specs/af-lane-0112.000.pdf
Multi-Protocol over ATM Version 1	ftp://ftp.atmforum.com/pub/approved-specs/af-mpoa-0087.000.pdf
LANE v2.0 LUNI Interface	ftp://ftp.atmforum.com/pub/approved-specs/af-lane-0084.000.pdf
Multi-Protocol over ATM Version 1.0 MIB	ftp://ftp.atmforum.com/pub/approved-specs/af-mpoa-0092.000.pdf
LAN Emulation Client Management Specification Version 2.0	ftp://ftp.atmforum.com/pub/approved-specs/af-lane-0093.000.pdf
LANE Servers Management Spec v1.0	ftp://ftp.atmforum.com/pub/approved-specs/af-lane-0057.000.pdf

Routing and Switching

ATM is an internetwork environment that uses layer 2 switching to move data around through network clouds. IP is an internetwork environment that uses layer 3 routing to move data around through network clouds. Trying to make them interoperate is a problem because each environment is designed to optimize the way data moves around its own network clouds. Consider Figure 9.1. An IP internetwork and an ATM internetwork may overlap in large part, but not entirely. Depending on how IP and ATM are made to interface, network traffic may be routed and switched suboptimally. In most cases, the IP network is the more comprehensive and larger, so we need not be as worried about carrying IP packets out of the IP network cloud and into the ATM-only portion of the ATM cloud. However, a bigger problem arises when we try to handle the routing of IP packets within the boundaries of an ATM cloud.

The problem occurs when you map an IP network architecture with subnets and routers onto an ATM network that may contain multiple IP

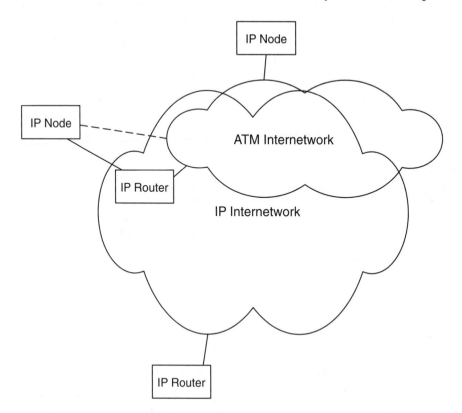

Figure 9.1 Overlapping internetworks.

routing domains. In these cases, packets can be routed unnecessarily from IP subnet to IP router to IP subnet, through the ATM cloud, when a direct, switched, path is available through the ATM cloud.

Using ATM for IP networks raises many routing issues, some of which we note in Chapter 12. However, the basic issue of figuring out ways to create shortcuts for IP packets through ATM clouds is addressed by the Next Hop Resolution Protocol (NHRP), defined in RFC 2332, "NBMA Next Hop Resolution Protocol (NHRP)," and supplemented by several other RFCs (see Table 9.3). We examine NHRP in greater detail in Chapter 12, as well as introduce the Multiprotocol Label Switching (MPLS) specification.

By mid 1999, the IETF MPLS working group was still laboring away at the specifications but had not yet gotten any of its Internet-Drafts approved as RFCs. MPLS defines a mechanism by which IP routing can be encapsulated and effectively bypassed (for performance purposes) for IP traffic that passes through ATM network clouds. This mechanism is introduced in Chapter 12.

Quality of Service

Even before the Internet Protocol as we know it (IPv4) was specified in RFC 791, back in 1981, the idea of treating some packets differently from others was a part of the Internet. IPv4 incorporates a type of service (ToS) field in its header, even though implementers have not found ways to put it to good use. The difficulty in implementing any kind of quality of service over a connectionless network protocol such as IP comes from the need to notify the network that a packet is related to some other packet or packets or stream of packets. Although IPv6 incorporates some enhancements to the idea of type of service, using the concept of flows, its success remains to be seen.

Table 9.3 Next Hop Resolution Protocol (NHRP) RFCs

RFC	TITLE
RFC 2332	NBMA Next Hop Resolution Protocol (NHRP)
RFC 2333	NHRP Protocol Applicability Statement
RFC 2336	Classical IP to NHRP Transition
RFC 2583	Guidelines for Next Hop Client (NHC) Developers

However, ATM is a connection-oriented technology and is ideally suited for implementing quality of service (QoS) differentiation. QoS and its partner, resource reservation, are quite easy under ATM: Stations signaling a connection not only negotiate a switched path between each other but also the terms by which that path will be maintained. Resource reservation, another sticky issue for connectionless IP, which can not even guarantee what route a packet will take between nodes, is also a fundamental feature of ATM.

Resource reservation, of course, is an important partner for quality of service. The QoS can vary by providing different priorities, and a guaranteed quality of service can be easily provided as long as it is possible to reserve bandwidth resources ahead of time. Although IP has done quite well so far with no guaranteed service, virtually all IP applications are variations on some form of either file transfer or terminal emulation. Downloading a Web page is more or less the same as downloading a file from an FTP server.

For more interesting applications, such as video conferencing, voice and telephony over IP, and any other application that requires significant bandwidth yet is sensitive to latency, resource reservation and quality of service issues must be resolved. IP over ATM holds promise for solving some of these problems. As we see in Chapter 13, "Managing Network Traffic," IP QoS and resource reservation present their own difficulties, as does the attempt to use ATM to help deploy these mechanisms. Table 9.4 lists some of the relevant RFCs related to quality of service and resource reservations.

Table 9.4 Quality of Service and Resource Reservation RFCs

RFC	TITLE
RFC 2386	A Framework for QoS-based Routing in the Internet
RFC 1821	Integration of Real-time Services in an IP-ATM Network Architecture
RFC 2170	Application REQuested IP over ATM (AREQUIPA)
RFC 2381	Interoperation of Controlled-Load Service and Guaranteed Service with ATM
RFC 2386	A Framework for QoS-based Routing in the Internet
RFC 2212	Specification of Guaranteed Quality of Service
RFC 2379	RSVP over ATM Implementation Guidelines
RFC 2380	RSVP over ATM Implementation Requirements
RFC 2381	Interoperation of Controlled-Load Service and Guaranteed Service with ATM
RFC 2382	A Framework for Integrated Services and RSVP over ATM

ATM and SNMP

As we discovered in Chapter 7, just about anything that is (or can be) connected to an IP network gets its own Management Information Base (MIB) definition. ATM is no exception, and we summarize the ATM and related MIBs as well as discuss how SNMP works with ATM in Chapter 14, "ATM Management."

Future Directions

At least for the next year or so, it is possible to map out the progress in Internet standards by checking out the working groups. Four working groups that are involved in ATM and related development are listed in Table 9.5. These four working groups are involved directly with ATM issues, though at various stages in their development. As we see in Chapter 15, "The Future of ATM and IP," considering the relative newness of ATM itself, it is not surprising that there is some uncertainty about the future directions of IP and ATM.

Reading List

There are many RFCs and other documents relevant to this chapter. If you are interested in understanding IP over ATM, you can start with the RFCs listed in Table 9.1. For more about LAN Emulation (LANE) as well as other ATM Forum specifications, Table 9.2 should provide a good start. RFCs relating to NHRP are listed in Table 9.3, while QoS and RSVP RFCs are listed in Table 9.4.

You may also want to visit the home pages for the IETF working groups whose work relates to ATM, listed in Table 9.5.

Finally, the ATM Forum website provides a good starting point for learning more about ATM specifications: www.atmforum.com.

Table 9.5   IETF Working Groups Pursuing ATM-Related Issues

WORKGROUP TITLE	URL
AToM MIB (atommib)	www.ietf.org/html.charters/atommib-charter.html
Multiprotocol Label Switching (mpls)	www.ietf.org/html.charters/mpls-charter.html
Internetworking Over NBMA (ion)	www.ietf.org/html.charters/ion-charter.html
Integrated Services (intserv)	www.ietf.org/html.charters/intserv-charter.html

Mapping IP onto ATM

In this chapter, we take a look at the initial efforts to map IP onto ATM. Classical IP and ARP over ATM or just plain IP over ATM (IPOA) takes the simple approach of dealing with ATM as if it were a link layer protocol. It defines mechanisms for encapsulating IP packets into ATM protocol data units, for deploying ATM networks as logical IP subnets, and for doing signaling through the ATM network via IP. Also defined are mechanisms for doing address resolution, broadcasts, and multicast over a network transport that does not easily support those functions.

In this chapter, we start by looking at multiprotocol encapsulation over ATM Adaptation Layer 5 (AAL5). This is how IP packets are turned into ATM PDUs. It also specifies two different encapsulation methods: One allows multiplexing of protocols over individual VCs, while the other uses a separate VC for each protocol.

From there, we continue with a discussion of Classical IP and ARP over ATM (IPOA), as described in RFC 2225. In particular, we focus on the use of the logical IP subnet (LIS) structure, issues relating to the default IP maximum transmission unit (MTU) over AAL5, how nodes signal each other to determine which other IP nodes are connected to PVCs, and address resolution issues. We finish the chapter by covering the mechanisms that allow ATM networks to support multicast and broadcast.

Multiprotocol Encapsulation over AAL5

RFC 1483, "Multiprotocol Encapsulation over ATM Adaptation Layer 5," does not change the way ATM PDUs are segmented and reassembled. (Segmentation and reassembly [SAR], which occurs in the lower part of the AAL layer, is covered in Chapter 8.) It simply describes how the ATM PDUs are incorporated into the payload of a Common Part Convergence Sublayer (CPCS) protocol data unit of the ATM Adaptation Layer type 5.

RFC 1483 describes two different methods for encapsulating connectionless network traffic, such as IP packets, over ATM Adaptation Layer 5. The first method permits different protocols to be multiplexed over one ATM VC. This is accomplished through the use of a prefixed IEEE 802.2 Logical Link Control (LLC) header. The LLC header, defined by the IEEE 802.2 standard, precedes and is part of the data being packaged into a layer 2 frame, and it provides information about the protocols being carried in the frame. An ATM station can receive transmissions of more than one protocol type from any other station and determine which protocol they belong to by parsing the LLC header. The other encapsulation method simply assigns a separate VC to each protocol in use. A station receives data on one VC that has been designated as carrying IP traffic, while receiving other types of traffic on other VCs.

These two different multiplexing mechanisms, LLC encapsulation and VC-based multiplexing, are useful in different situations. In ATM networks that make extensive use of permanent VCs (PVCs) because switched VCs are not easy to set up or because using multiple SVCs is costly, LLC encapsulation makes sense. It allows sharing of existing resources. On the other hand, as long as SVCs are easy to set up and don't cost too much (either in money or setup time), VC-based multiplexing makes more sense. Configuring the chosen method is done by hand when PVCs are being used and is done as a part of the signaling process between two stations when an SVC is set up.

To return to the AAL5 protocol data unit discussed in Chapter 8, "Asynchronous Transfer Mode," consider Figure 10.1, which is taken from RFC 1483. The payload itself can be as long as 65,535 bytes, followed by pad bits to ensure the PDU payload evenly fits into 48-byte ATM cell payloads. The CPCS encapsulation is done through the padding and a trailer, which includes four fields.

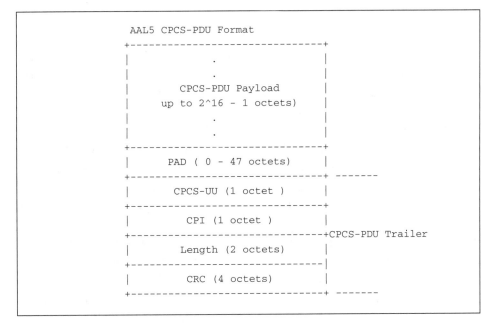

```
AAL5 CPCS-PDU Format
+-----------------------------+
|              .              |
|              .              |
|        CPCS-PDU Payload      |
|      up to 2^16 - 1 octets)  |
|              .              |
|              .              |
+-----------------------------+
|      PAD ( 0 - 47 octets)   |
+-----------------------------+ -------
|      CPCS-UU (1 octet )     |
+-----------------------------+
|        CPI (1 octet )       |
+-----------------------------+CPCS-PDU Trailer
|      Length (2 octets)      |
+-----------------------------|
|        CRC (4 octets)       |
+-----------------------------+ -------
```

Figure 10.1   AAL5 Common Part Convergence Sublayer PDU (from RFC 1483).

The CPCS PDU encapsulation fields, in addition to the pad and payload fields, include the following:

User-to-User, or CPCS-UU, field. This one-byte field can be used to transfer CPCS user-to-user information, but it is not used with RFC 1483 encapsulation and can be safely ignored.

Common Part Indicator (CPI) field. Originally intended to be used for bit-alignment, this one-byte field is not used in AAL5.

Length. This two-byte field contains an integer indicating the length in bytes of the Payload field.

CRC. This is a cyclic redundancy check on the entire CPSC PDU, exclusive of the CRC field itself.

The rest of this section summarizes the two different encapsulation methods. In general, LLC encapsulation is used more often. LLC encapsulation support is required and is the default mechanism for AAL5 encapsulation.

LLC Encapsulation

As mentioned earlier, LLC encapsulation is used when more than one protocol is to be carried over a single VC (it does not matter whether it is a permanent or switched VC). To make this work, the payload field of the AAL5 PDU has to contain some more information about what it is carrying. The LLC header, as defined in IEEE 802.2, provides a facility for identifying the contents of a protocol data unit payload. In addition to the LLC header, a Sub-Network Access Protocol (SNAP) header (also defined in IEEE 802.2) is often also included.

The LLC prefix is three bytes long, with three single-byte fields. Destination Service Access Point (DSAP) and Source Service Access Point (SSAP) refer to the upper-layer protocol used for the data being encapsulated, and the Control field can be used for administration by some protocols but for LLC encapsulation this field is always given the value 0x03.

The SNAP header was defined because it was thought that 8 bits would not be enough to identify all possible encapsulated protocols, so two additional header fields are added, bringing the total SNAP/LLC header to 8 bytes. Because SNAP replaces the one-byte LLC header service access point (SAP) fields with a more specific identifier, the presence of a SNAP header is indicated by putting the value of 0xAA in the DSAP and SSAP fields. Because IP datagrams must be identified by a SNAP header, LLC encapsulations of IP datagrams will always have the hexadecimal value 0xAA-AA-03.

The SNAP header consists of two additional fields, the Organizationally Unique Identifier (OUI) and the Ethertype. The (OUI) is a three-byte value that identifies the organization that administers the value found in the two-byte Protocol Identifier (PID) field. The PID field identifies encapsulated protocol. Figure 10.2 shows how an IPv4 datagram would be encapsulated into AAL5, per RFC 1483. Note that the EtherType

```
        +-------------------------------+
        |      LLC   0xAA-AA-03          |
        +-------------------------------+
        |      OUI 0x00-00-00           |
        +-------------------------------+
        |      EtherType 0x08-00        |
        +-------------------------------+
        |              .                |
        |                               |
        |          IPv4  PDU            |
        |      (up to 2^16 - 9 octets)  |
        |              .                |
        +-------------------------------+
```

Figure 10.2   LLC Encapsulation of an IPv4 packet (from RFC 1483).

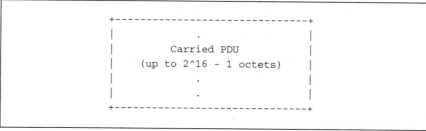

```
        +-------------------------------+
        |                 .             |
        |           Carried PDU         |
        |        (up to 2^16 - 1 octets)|
        |                 .             |
        |                               |
        |                 .             |
        +-------------------------------+
```

Figure 10.3   VC-based Multiplexing (from RFC 1483).

0x08-00 is in the PID field. This value identifies the contents as an IPv4 datagram. A value in this field of 0x08-06 indicates an ARP message. Other EtherType values are permitted (see IANA for more information about EtherTypes).

Because the extra overhead from the IEEE 802.2 LLC/SNAP encapsulation is only 8 bytes (AAL5 PDUs are usually in the 8Kb range), it adds minimally to the cost of doing LLC encapsulation instead of VC-based multiplexing. LLC encapsulation is necessary in some situations, but it can be used to good advantage even where SVCs are easy and cheap.

VC-Based Multiplexing

Because VC-based multiplexing uses a single protocol for each VC, there is no need to identify the protocol being carried in AAL5 PDUs. The sending and receiving ATM stations already know what protocol is in use because either the protocol was manually configured when the VC was set up or the two stations negotiated it dynamically during the signaling process. Figure 10.3 shows the typical payload containing an IPv4 packet. Obviously, the AAL5 PDU consists entirely of the payload.

Updating RFC 1483

The Internetworking over NBMA (ion) working group of the IETF is actively working on an update to replace RFC 1483. It will clarify the existing document and will probably add discussion of LLC/SNAP encapsulation of Virtual Private Network (VPN) data. This kind of VPN refers not to the transfer of encrypted data across the Internet between nodes or sites, but rather the use of a public ATM network to carry private organizational data between sites or campuses.

Applying Multiprotocol Encapsulation

The update to RFC 1483 enumerates some of the areas in which multiprotocol encapsulation is applied to real networking tasks. Taken from the work in progress, these applications include the following:

- Multiprotocol encapsulation enables point-to-point links between routers and bridges across ATM networks. A PVC, manually configured, can be used to provide a point-to-point link carrying multiprotocol traffic in these cases.

- An ATM network that behaves like a logical IP subnet (LIS) can carry IP and other types of datagrams using multiprotocol encapsulation described in RFC 1483 for Classical IP over ATM (RFC 2225).

- The ATM Forum's LAN Emulation (LANE) specification can use multiprotocol encapsulation (LANE is described in Chapter 11).

- The Next Hop Resolution Protocol (NHRP) described in Chapter 12 uses multiprotocol encapsulation to provide shortcuts through very large ATM networks that are too large to behave as logical subnets and still perform adequately.

- Another ATM Forum specification, Multiprotocol over ATM (MPOA), integrates LANE and NHRP and takes advantage of multiprotocol encapsulation to create a generic bridging/routing environment.

- IP multicast, as defined in RFC 2022 and using a multicast address resolution server (MARS), utilizes multiprotocol encapsulation for transporting multicast datagrams to recipients in an ATM network.

- PPP over ATM is possible using the extensions described in RFC 2364, "PPP Over AAL5," and multiprotocol encapsulation.

Clearly, multiprotocol encapsulation is fundamental to most aspects of IP networking over ATM.

Classical IP and ARP over ATM

Several important factors must be considered when deploying IP over a link layer protocol:

- Formatting and encapsulating IP packets for transmission over the link layer

- Structuring the link layer under IP

- Determining the maximum transmission unit size for the local link and for the entire path
- Associating a link layer address with an IP address and vice versa
- Dealing with the lack of native multicast/broadcast support

Originally specified for the standards-track in 1994 in RFC 1577, "Classical IP and ARP over ATM," the basic approach to IP over ATM treats ATM as if it were a link layer protocol and simply maps ATM networks into the same type of architectures used by traditional LANs and backbones. RFC 2225 retains the name but updates the content and incorporates material that was previously documented in RFC 1626, "Default IP MTU for Use over ATM AAL5."

We already know how the first item raised in this list is handled: IP packets over ATM are encapsulated in AAL5 PDUs using the LLC/SNAP multiprotocol encapsulation described earlier in this chapter and in RFC 1483. We discuss each of these items next.

Logical IP Subnets

Organizations gain experience with ATM largely by using it to replace other existing networks. This might mean replacing an FDDI backbone with an ATM backbone or replacing an Ethernet local area network with an ATM local area network. In these instances, ATM can be viewed simply as a different type of link layer communication medium, and a one-to-one correspondence between running IP over ATM and running IP over the older communication medium is desirable. Thus, Classical IP over ATM makes a great deal of sense for situations like those demonstrated in Figure 10.4, where an existing network structure maps directly to the new structure. In this case, the hosts are all connected to the Ethernet in an IP subnet, and when the conversion to ATM is complete, the same hosts are all connected to the same IP subnet via an ATM network.

Figure 10.4 demonstrates that for simple upgrades, the rest of the network architecture can be preserved. However, an unstated assumption that the ATM network stands alone and links no stations or networks other than those shown in the figure is made here. We've mentioned the term logical IP subnet (LIS) before, and this is what is meant: The LIS consists of a set of IP hosts, servers, and a router that functions as if it were an IP subnet. In practice, there may be more than one LIS connected to the same ATM network. Figure 10.5 shows what happens when two IP subnets deployed on two separate Ethernet segments and

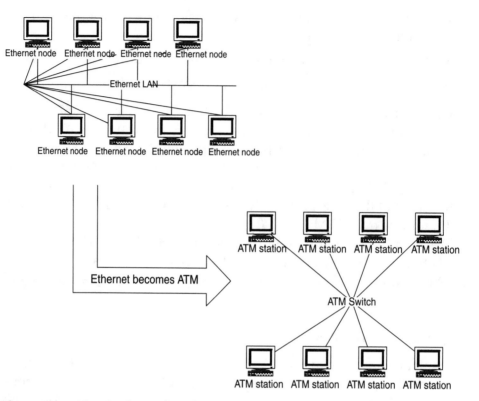

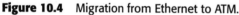

Figure 10.4 Migration from Ethernet to ATM.

linked by a router are converted to ATM. The new ATM network is represented as a cloud. It might be a single ATM switch or it might be an ATM WAN—it does not matter which. All IP nodes are attached to the ATM network, all retaining their original IP subnet numbering. There are two subnets and a single router, as there was before, but instead of two networks connected only by a router, there is now only a single network cloud to which all nodes are attached. IP packets originating on network A must be routed through the router to get to network B. There is no way (at least not using Classical IP over ATM) to move a packet directly from a node on network A to a node on network B.

RFC 2225 defines configuration requirements for the LIS first by specifying requirements for IP hosts and routers, then by specifying the set of ATM parameters that must be implemented on each IP station connected to the ATM network. First, the host IP node configuration requirements (adapted from RFC 2225) are these:

- All LIS members must have the same IP network/subnet number and address mask.

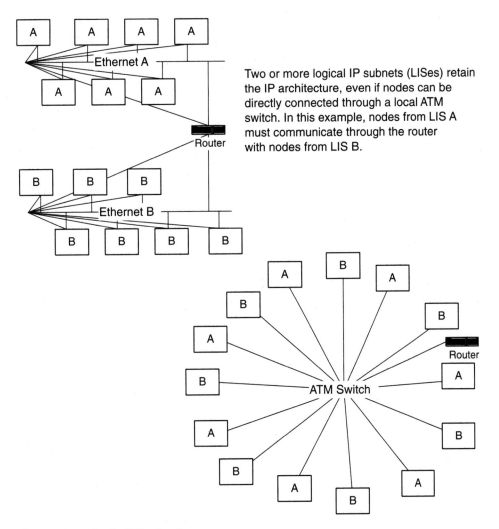

Two or more logical IP subnets (LISes) retain the IP architecture, even if nodes can be directly connected through a local ATM switch. In this example, nodes from LIS A must communicate through the router with nodes from LIS B.

Figure 10.5   Logical IP subnets.

- All LIS members *must* be directly connected to the ATM network.
- All LIS members *must* be able to resolve IP addresses to ATM addresses via ATMARP and vice versa via InATMARP when using SVCs. (We cover ATMARP and InATMARP in the next section.)
- All LIS members *must* be able to resolve VCs to IP addresses via InATMARP when using PVCs.
- All LIS members *must* be able to communicate via ATM with all other members in the same LIS, that is, the Virtual Connection topology underlying the intercommunication among the members is fully meshed.

In addition, each individual IP station must be configured with its own ATM hardware address, which acts as a hardware address for the purposes of address resolution, and with an ATMARP Request Address list. This is a list of the ATM addresses of at least one ATMARP server located in the IP station's own LIS.

When there is more than one LIS reachable in an ATM network (in other words, when there are two or more LISs present in a single ATM network, as shown in Figure 10.5), any router serving one LIS should also be able to interconnect with other LISs in that ATM network. Any router that serves more than one LIS must support a separate set of LIS parameters for each individual LIS. Thus, the router in Figure 10.5 must have two sets of parameters, one for each LIS it links.

Configuring IP over ATM like this means that it is relatively easy to migrate non-ATM networks to ATM networks. However, it is less simple to deal with more organically developed ATM networks that may span multiple logical IP subnets.

Maximum Transmission Unit (MTU) and ATM

Another issue raised as networks are converted to ATM is that of the maximum transmission unit (MTU) size. All link layer protocols have an absolute maximum size of protocol data unit they can carry, but there is usually a lower size limit defined so that the frames carried on one link layer don't have to be fragmented as soon as they hit a different link layer on a neighboring network hop.

ATM may transmit data in 53 byte cells, but its PDU size can be considerably larger—up to 65,535 bytes long. The maximum transmission unit (MTU) is defined as the largest size that a protocol data unit can be without causing encapsulated protocol data units to be fragmented. In general, the bigger the better. For one thing, larger packets mean smaller proportional overhead for the protocol headers. If the protocol headers take up 20 bytes (as in most IP packets), a 200-byte payload would have a 10% overhead, while a 20,000-byte payload would have only 0.1% overhead. Also, network devices such as routers expend almost as many resources processing a short packet as they do processing a long one.

RFC 2225 discusses choosing a default MTU for ATM AAL5. One common bandwidth-intensive application, the Network File System (NFS), is noted as using a frame size of 8192 bytes and is offered as an example of the type of application whose PDUs should not be fragmented. Thus, the MTU for IP over AAL5 should be at least 8192 bytes. Add about a hundred or so bytes for UDP, IP, and LLC headers, and you come up with the value of 8300 bytes.

The RFC also cites the default MTU defined for Switched Multimegabit Data Services (SMDS), another high-speed networking technology, whose MTU is 9180 bytes (see RFC 1209, "The Transmission of IP Datagrams over the SMDS Service"). Considering that SMDS and ATM often interoperate, the RFC authors reason that the IP over ATM MTU should be the same: 9180 bytes. This easily accommodates NFS frames and smoothes the integration with other networks.

All implementations over PVCs must use the default value of 9180 bytes for the MTU. However, when using SVCs, the stations are permitted to negotiate a smaller or larger MTU, depending on what the two nodes determine is appropriate.

Address Resolution

How does an IP station know where to send packets on its directly connected network? It must use some mechanism to resolve an IP address into a local network address. This is relatively simple in, for example, Ethernet networks where a node can broadcast a message asking, in essence, "Hey, where is IP address W.X.Y.Z?" The node having that IP address notes the network media access control (MAC) address of the requesting node and sends back a message saying, essentially, "That's me. Here's my MAC address." As these exchanges go on, other hosts on the same network listen to the broadcasts and make a note of the IP and MAC addresses of anyone sending a request and of anyone sending a reply. All of these values are copied into a cache, which the nodes can then consult any time they need to look up another node. If the address they seek is not there, they can submit their own request to the network.

That, in a paragraph, is what the Address Resolution Protocol (ARP) is all about. ARP is specified in RFC 826 (STD 37), "An Ethernet Address Resolution Protocol — or — Converting Network Protocol Addresses to 48.bit Ethernet Address for Transmission on Ethernet Hardware." ARP uses UDP to send very simply formatted request and response messages. As defined for Ethernet, an ARP request asks for a 6-byte MAC address associated with a 4-byte IP address. The protocol itself can be adapted to other size addresses, but as defined in RFC 826, it depends on the use of broadcasts to be able to query all connected nodes so that all connected nodes can eavesdrop on other nodes making queries and keep track of the results in their own ARP caches.

A different problem occurs at times in IP networks: A node is connected to another node through the link layer and knows the link layer address but not the IP address of the node at the other end. This problem occurs anywhere a networked station has a virtual connection to another station but does not have the other station's IP address. It occurs in Frame Relay networks and was the motivation for the Inverse ARP protocol extension defined in RFC 1293, "Inverse Address Resolution Protocol." The same situation can happen in ATM networks where PVCs are in use.

ATMARP

As we've mentioned, ATM does not support broadcasts. Every time data is to be transmitted across an ATM network, it requires the creation of an SVC or the use of an existing PVC. In either case, sending the same message to every station on an ATM network can become costly in time and resources. This means that doing ARP under ATM can be a problem.

The solution to this problem is to require every IP subnet on an ATM network to include a node that acts as an ARP server. If a node supports SVCs, it can not know ATM addresses for any other nodes on the switched part of the network. It must, however, be configured with the address of at least ATMARP server. Every station in the LIS must use the same ATMARP service, which must authoritatively resolve all requests by LIS members.

ATMARP servers are passive rather than active in gathering ARP data. A requesting station sends an ATMARP request (of the same form as a regular ARP request) directly to the ATMARP server, using an LLC/SNAP encapsulated packet. When it receives such a request, the ATMARP server parses the incoming ARP information, notes the VC on which the request came in, and stores it all in case another IP node later requests address resolution information for that IP node. The server then checks its ARP table for the requested IP address and responds appropriately. Appropriate responses depend on what happens when the ATMARP server checks its table. For example, one response is to report to server management if the source IP address is the same as the IP address for which an ATM address is being requested and sending the data from its ARP table to the requesting node.

If the source IP address is the same as the IP address for which an ATM address is being requested, but there is no current entry in the ATMARP table for that IP address, the server must open a new table entry with the information provided in the request. This is actually how IP nodes announce themselves to the network and is one method of keeping all IP addresses unique.

When the requesting node is actually asking for an ATM address for a different station, it checks its table and sends the requested information (if it is in there) or sends a negative reply (if there is no entry for that IP address). The ATMARP server does not do anything to seek out a missing node: It only listens. In this way, it keeps network traffic lower. Since each IP node announces itself to the network with an ARP request (actually, the nodes are checking to make sure that the IP address they think they should have is actually not already being used by some other node), the ATMARP server logs each and every IP node as it comes onto the network.

ARP table entries do not remain valid indefinitely. They expire in a matter of minutes, so clients must not only notify the ATMARP server for an initial registration but also must periodically refresh their table entries so that other nodes can reach them. RFC 2225 specifies that clients MUST refresh their entries at least every 15 minutes. There are more details to the ATMARP specification, covering issues like handling entry expirations and additional interactions between client and server, ATMARP packet formats and fields, and more. These are all available in RFC 2225.

Inverse ARP

If all your circuits are switched, then by definition you don't know the link layer address for your destination and you've got to use ATMARP to figure out how to connect to an IP address. On the other hand, with PVCs, you're dealing with the equivalent of a hard-wired connection from one station to another. Stations that use only PVCs must at some point be configured with the ATM address of the station at the other end. Since this is all to do with ATM and nothing to do with the higher-layer protocols, there is no reason to query the other end for an IP address. This is where InATMARP comes in.

Inverse ARP as defined in RFC 1293 was adopted for InATMARP. RFC 2390, "Inverse Address Resolution Protocol," is a draft standard that makes RFC 1293 obsolete. InATMARP is required for stations using only PVCs. (By the same token, ATMARP is irrelevant for such a station.) All IP nodes are required to be able to respond to an InATMARP request with an IP address. InATMARP messages use the standard ARP format, with fields for link layer address and IP address for both the requesting station and the replying station.

Multicast and Broadcast

Multicast and broadcast, in the way those terms are understood for classical IP, just don't happen under ATM. Yes, it is possible to set up point-to-multipoint circuits under ATM, but it's hardly as cheap or as easy to do as a multicast over a medium that inherently supports broadcasts as Ethernet does. ATM is connection oriented, which means that a station has to know every station that wants to receive a multicast or every station connected to the network in order to send out a broadcast. Neither of these things is easily knowable in an ATM environment, which calls for a special solution.

IP Multicast

IP multicast, defined in RFC 1112, "Host Extensions for IP Multicasting," allows IP nodes to join a multicast group if they want to receive packets addressed to the multicast address associated with that group. In theory, it's kind of like tuning in to a cable television station: You only get it if you select it.

Layer 2 multicast on an Ethernet can be relatively simple, because joining a group simply means listening for frames sent to the multicast group address out on the broadcast medium. Doing IP multicast, where any IP node can join any multicast group, can be more complicated.

For one thing, not all layer 2 networks support multicast as easily as Ethernet. For another, you've got to have the cooperation of routers to do multicast in routed IP networks. What happens is that an IP node wishing to join a multicast group would notify its router that it wishes to join the group. That router then has to forward that join request (actually, it tells its router that it wants to join the group). Assuming that all routers in an internetwork can support multicast, the routers whose clients want to be members of the group simply transmit multicast packets to the layer 2 multicast address (for Ethernet, anyway) associated on the local network with the IP multicast address.

Things get more complicated in connection-oriented networks, such as ATM, which we cover next.

Multicast over ATM

RFC 2022, "Support for Multicast over UNI 3.0/3.1 based ATM Networks," defines such a mechanism: the Multicast Address Resolution Server (MARS). Very simply, a MARS acts very much like an ATM ARP server. A MARS keeps track of IP multicast addresses and the ATM interfaces of the stations that are members of the multicast group. When a station wishes to join or leave a multicast group, it informs the MARS of its request. The MARS acts on the station's behalf, relaying multicast requests to the appropriate stations and passing along multicast packets to the stations that have requested them.

RFC 2022 scrupulously avoids specifying a layer 3 protocol, such as IP, though we're most interested with the way a MARS would work in an IP over ATM network. MARS, as defined in RFC 2022, makes it possible to do intranetwork layer 3 multicasting over ATM: Nodes on the ATM network can communicate with multiple nodes in a simulation of the kind of layer 2 multicast that is possible with Ethernet. Two mechanisms are cited, one that uses meshes of point-to-multipoint VCs and the other one using ATM level multicast servers (MCS). We cover both later in this section. First, let's discuss how a MARS serves ATM stations in an ATM network.

Multicast Cluster

RFC 2022 specifies that each MARS manages a "cluster" of stations attached to the ATM network, with "cluster" defined as those ATM interfaces that have chosen to participate in direct ATM connections to achieve multicasting among themselves within the ATM network. This effectively means that a cluster consists of those endpoints that have chosen to use the same MARS for registration of multicast memberships.

This also means that when multicast traffic traverses clusters, the packets must pass through an "intercluster device"—in other words, an IP router (assuming that we're using IP for layer 3 here).

Another point to ponder is that while the task of assigning ATM stations to a MARS is left to the network administrator, each logical IP subnet (LIS) must be served by its own, separate MARS. This means that a MARS cluster potentially has the same membership as the LIS it serves. This is only a potential membership, because RFC 2022 specifies that only those stations actively using the MARS are considered cluster members.

Intracluster Multicast

There are two approaches to doing multicast transmissions among stations on an ATM network. One is to allow each station that is going to be sending multicast packets to set up a point-to-multipoint VC. This type of VC is often referred to as a tree with a set of leaf nodes (receiving nodes). When there is only one sender and multiple recipients (one station sends data while the rest listen silently), this is just a tree. This approach to multicast becomes a VC mesh when more than one station transmits to the multicast group. Because each sending node is both an originator and a group member, it has a set of leaves (that are listening to its transmissions) and is a leaf on at least one other tree. Figure 10.6 clarifies how this works and also demonstrates why such an approach might not be optimal as networks and multicast groups grow. The need for many VCs grows quickly as the number of members grows.

A different approach to intracluster multicast is to use a multicast server (MCS). In this approach, an MCS is designated to take care of all the multicast activity for everyone on the cluster. All group members send their multicast transmissions to the MCS, and the MCS maintains a single point-to-multipoint VC to all the group members. Figure 10.7

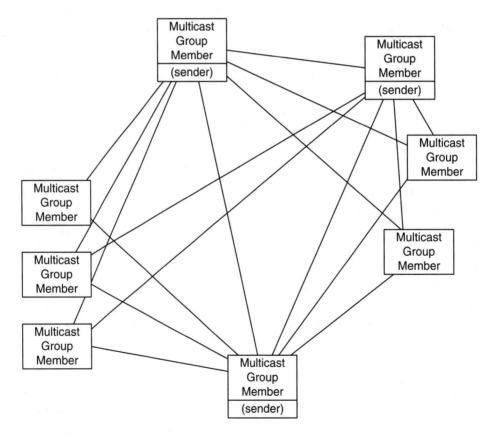

Figure 10.6 The VC mesh approach to intracluster multicasting.

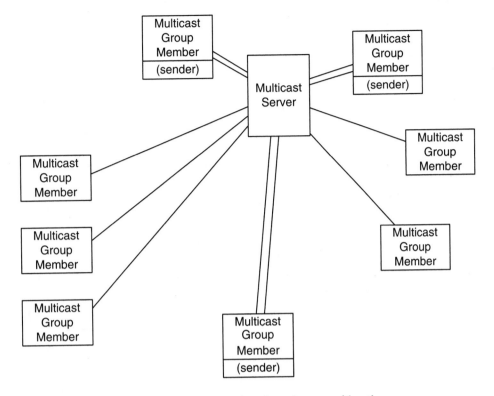

Figure 10.7   The multicast server approach to intracluster multicasting.

illustrates the multicast server approach to intracluster multicasting. Stations that are sending to the multicast group have a point-to-point VC to the MCS, which relays all multicast packets to all members of the group.

Although the MCS approach is a more economical and more elegant solution to the problem, the VC mesh approach is simpler and has been designated the default mechanism to be used for handling intracluster multicast.

Broadcast over ATM

Multicast and broadcast can be viewed as functionally identical. A broadcast address is simply a multicast address to which all nodes on a network are members; a multicast address is simply a broadcast address whose subscribers can opt in or out of. RFC 2226, "IP Broadcast over ATM Networks," simply extends the MARS approach described in RFC 2022 and applies it to broadcast. Under RFC 2226, all nodes register as members of the broadcast group with the MARS serving the nodes' LIS. Again, the VC mesh mechanism for distributing multicast is the default approach for broadcast. Broadcasts can also be carried through an MCS, and this is likely to be the more appropriate solution inasmuch as a VC mesh approach tends to tax ATM switches and VC resources when a broadcast is being distributed.

IPv6 over ATM

The Internet Protocol has been undergoing renovations since the early 1990s, and standards for the next version of IP— IPv6—are fairly stable. Of course, this means that specifications for running IPv6 over ATM must also be created. RFC 2492, "IPv6 over ATM Networks," relies on the work done in RFC 2491, "IPv6 over Non-Broadcast Multiple Access (NBMA) networks." Both are proposed standards.

The biggest change for IP over ATM under IPv6 relates to the use of neighbor discovery (ND), which changes the way address resolution is accomplished. RFC 2461, "Neighbor Discovery for IP Version 6 (IPv6)," is the draft standard that documents this mechanism. Comparing functions performed in IPv4, neighbor discovery is used instead of ARP and also replaces the ICMP router discovery and ICMP redirect functions. IPv6 over ATM still relies on most of the same mechanisms as IPv4 over ATM, such as MARS.

Reading List

The two most important RFCs to study for this chapter are RFC 1483, "Multiprotocol Encapsulation over ATM Adaptation Layer 5," and RFC 2225, "Classical IP and ARP over ATM." Other related RFCs are mentioned in passing in the text of the chapter. RFCs that define the specifications related to address resolution under IP are listed in Table 10.1. RFCs related to multicast and broadcast in ATM networks are listed in Table 10.2.

Table 10.1 Address Resolution Specifications

RFC	TITLE
RFC 826 (STD 37)	An Ethernet Address Resolution Protocol — or — Converting Network Protocol Addresses to 48.bit Ethernet Address for Transmission on Ethernet Hardware
RFC 2390	Inverse Address Resolution Protocol

Table 10.1 *(Continued)*

RFC	TITLE
RFC 2225	Classical IP and ARP over ATM
RFC 2601	ILMI-based Server Discovery for ATMARP

Table 10.2 ATM Multicast and Broadcast RFCs

RFC	TITLE
RFC 2022	Support for Multicast over UNI 3.0/3.1 based ATM Networks
RFC 2226	IP Broadcast over ATM Networks
RFC 2443	A Distributed MARS Service Using SCSP
RFC 2149	Multicast Server Architectures for MARS-based ATM multicasting
RFC 2121	Issues affecting MARS Cluster Size
RFC 2602	ILMI-based Server Discovery for MARS

The ATM Forum Solutions

Networking with ATM is fundamentally different from the data communications networks most organizations are accustomed to. With Token Ring or Ethernet networks, you can pretty much install an adapter card, plug a system into the network, and you're all set to start communicating across the LAN. The IETF approach to Classical IP over ATM, in which IP interfaces into ATM, treats ATM as if it were another link layer technology. IPOA works nicely as long as IP is the only protocol running over ATM. It looks down into the protocol stack and adapts IP downward to fit into ATM.

A different approach is to adapt ATM upward to make it behave like any other link layer technology and to make it usable by any protocol stack as if it were any other link layer technology. This is the approach taken by the ATM Forum with its LAN Emulation (LANE) and related specifications. The idea is to add on a layer on top of ATM to make it behave as if it is a regular Ethernet or Token Ring LAN. By making it possible for an ATM station to interface with applications through regular protocol stacks, migration from Ethernet or Token Ring networks to ATM networks is simplified.

One drawback to LANE, by itself, is that it can operate only in a bridged environment. In other words, it really acts as if it were a layer 2 network technology. Emulated LANs can be connected only through bridges. If you want to exit an emulated LAN you must do so by a router, even if the router passes the data along to another emulated LAN in the same ATM network cloud. The Multi-Protocol over ATM (MPOA) integrates the Next Hop Resolution Protocol (NHRP, discussed in Chapter 12, "IP Routing through ATM") with LANE, keeping the benefits of doing LAN emulation while at the same time allowing intersubnet transmission without getting routers involved.

In this chapter, we look briefly at the ATM Forum standards LAN Emulation (LANE) and Multi-Protocol over ATM (MPOA), and how they work with IP.

LAN Emulation

ATM is a sophisticated data communications technology, but it was originally designed for telecommunications rather than data networks. Although ATM has many benefits and advantages, it is an entirely new technology compared to Ethernet and Token Ring, and many organizations are still experimenting with it. Changing an organizational network infrastructure is an expensive proposition, and the ATM Forum determined that it would be useful to provide a LAN emulation service that would make it easier to bring in and integrate ATM into an organization's infrastructure.

Most data traffic within organizations is carried over local area networks, predominantly Ethernet/IEEE 802.3 and to a lesser extent Token Ring (IEEE 802.5) LANs. As we've mentioned before, there are significant differences between these LAN technologies and ATM. For one thing, LANs provide connectionless connectivity for messages. This means no explicit creation of a circuit between communicating nodes. All nodes are connected to the network, and all nodes are therefore able to freely send messages among themselves.

Another important difference between LANs and ATM is support for multicast and broadcast. We've already seen (in Chapter 10, "Mapping IP onto ATM") how important layer 2 multicast and broadcast support is to IP multicast and broadcast functions. Simulating those functions in a connection-oriented network environment such as ATM can be complicated.

Finally, LANs assign unique media access control (MAC) addresses to each network interface device. These addresses are independent of the network topology and are used by LAN software to direct network messages to the intended recipient. These are the 48-bit addresses that the Address Resolution Protocol (ARP) correlates with IP addresses. These are the addresses that the network protocol stack uses to address messages as they exit the system and are sent across the local link.

LANs are useful constructs, despite their limitations. For example, they tend to be limited in number of nodes and area over which they can be implemented. However, they are really good for sharing data among groups of computers, and LANs are deployed just about everywhere. Much of the existing network infrastructure is organized into LANs, and much of the existing network and network application software is designed to be used in a LAN environment. For ATM to *not* support a LAN infrastructure would put it at a great disadvantage when compared with other networking technologies.

The ATM Forum decided to build the LAN Emulation (LANE) service to fit on top of ATM to emulate the type of services that existing LANs provide across an ATM network, supported through a software layer in networked systems. With LANE, networked systems including user workstations, network servers, network bridges, and other devices can all be connected to an ATM network, but the software running on those nodes interacts with the network as if it were a traditional LAN. This approach also makes possible the interoperable bridging of ATM networks with traditional LANs, so that an Ethernet or Token Ring LAN can be connected to an ATM network. (Only an Ethernet or Token Ring LAN can be bridged to a LANE network; to connect an ATM network to Ethernet and Token Ring at the same means that one of the links must be through a layer 3 router while the other can be bridged.)

What Needs to Be Emulated

LANs have different attributes that can be emulated under ATM, and it is possible to be selective about which attributes are included in an emulation. The characteristics of a LAN that are cited in ATM Forum specifications for LAN Emulation include a MAC service emulation, which includes the encapsulation of MAC frames. In other words, network data is encapsulated into network frames in the same way that data in encapsulated into Ethernet or Token Ring frames. The frames have headers and trailers as defined in IEEE 802.x specifications for Ethernet/IEEE 802.3 and Token Ring (IEEE 802.5).

Specific LAN characteristics that are a part of the LANE standard include the following:

Connectionless Services. Under LANE, connected nodes behave as if it were unnecessary to establish an ATM connection—as if the node is connected to a shared network medium such as Ethernet or Token Ring. Setting up and using VCs is done under the covers, out of sight of the nodes' upper layer network applications.

Multicast Services. The LANE service supports multicast MAC addresses, just like Ethernet or Token Ring. Under LANE, nodes can send and receive data to and from layer 2 addresses signifying multicast groups, standard functional multicast addresses (such as "all local switches"), and broadcast, as if they were connected to a shared-access medium.

MAC Driver Interfaces in ATM Stations. Instead of creating network protocol stacks customized for each and every network interface card, modern protocol stacks are built to interface with the network interface through a standard software interface. The network interface vendors are responsible for building a piece of software for each of their interface cards that can communicate through these standard software interfaces. Three such interfaces for MAC device drivers are the Network Driver Interface Specification (NDIS), Open Data-Link Interface (ODI), and the Data Link Provider Interface (DLPI) specifications. LANE provides interfaces to these standard interfaces so that upper-layer protocols and applications can access the ATM network through the same type of protocol stack interaction as they use in real LANs.

Emulated LANs

Under LANE, an emulated LAN (or ELAN) can emulate either an Ethernet or a Token Ring LAN segment over a switched ATM network. According to the ATM Forum specifications, the ELAN is functionally identical to the emulated LAN type for applications running on attached nodes. A node attached to an ELAN is called a LAN Emulation Client (LE Client, or LEC). An ELAN consists of a collection of these LECs, all of which can set up direct connections with each other over the ATM network.

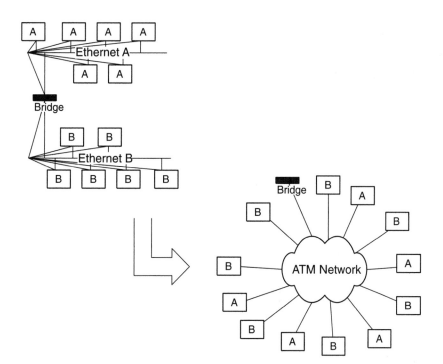

Figure 11.1   Migrating LANs to ELANs under ATM.

Stations connected to the same ATM network can belong to different ELANs. For example, if several Ethernet LANs were migrated to ATM, the LAN architecture might be retained even though all nodes are now connected to the same ATM cloud. Figure 11.1 shows a set of stations connected to the same ATM network, with all systems connected to the same network cloud.

Just as an end system can have more than one network interface and be connected to more than one LAN (routers, for example), so too can end systems be members of more than one ELAN. As Figure 11.1 shows, more than one ELAN can be configured on the same ATM network. This distinction is important, as it means that broadcasts are distributed only within an ELAN and not to all end systems connected to the ATM network. As the figure also shows, since the two Ethernet LANs are migrated to two separate ELANs, connectivity between the ELANs must still be maintained through a bridge.

Another implication of this retention of LAN characteristics is that you can bridge an ATM network into a legacy LAN in the same way you can bridge two ELANs together. Figure 11.2 shows how this looks. The LANE bridge has an interface on one side into the ATM cloud and a

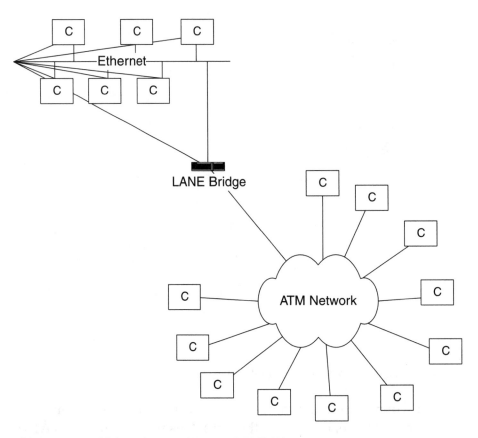

Figure 11.2   Bridging a legacy LAN to an ATM ELAN.

regular Ethernet interface on the other side. Inside the bridge, it does typical layer 2 bridge things, that is, it listens on each side for traffic that is destined for the other side.

When a broadcast frame is transmitted on the real Ethernet, the bridge reproduces that broadcast for the ELAN on the ATM cloud. When a frame, originating on the ELAN, is intended for a host on the Ethernet side, the frame gets sent to the bridge on the ATM network. The bridge then resends the frame on the Ethernet side. We see how LANE manages such bridging later in this chapter.

Benefits of LAN Emulation

As with IPOA, LANE tends not to take advantage of many of the benefits of ATM: It effectively turns a sophisticated internetworking technology into a LAN emulator. However, LANE is intended to reduce the cost of migrating to ATM by keeping existing LAN topologies in place, retaining compatibility with network application software, and being able to use bridges to allow phased migration from LAN to ATM.

LAN Emulation (LANE)

Figure 11.2 is functionally accurate, but it is not complete. It shows how an ELAN and a real LAN can be bridged, but it leaves out the all-important details that make it possible for an ELAN to function over ATM and with real LANs. These details are embodied in the LAN Emulation User Network Interface (LUNI v2), documented in the ATM Forum specification AF-LANE-0084.00. Very broadly, LANE mandates that each emulated LAN (ELAN) consists of a set of LAN Emulation Clients (LECs) and a single LAN Emulation Service (LE Service). Figure 11.3 shows what this looks like. LANE interactions are mediated through the services provided by the LE Service.

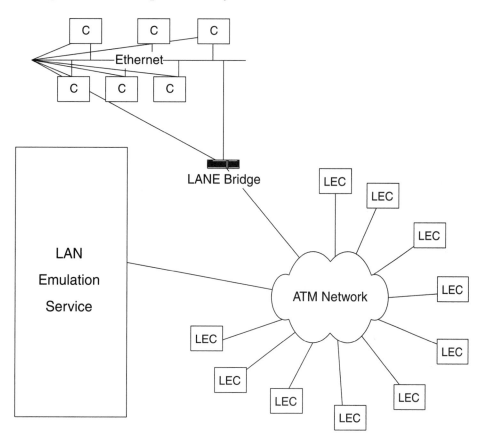

Figure 11.3   LAN Emulation Service (LE Service).

Within the ELAN, the LECs use the LES to interact with each other and with other ELAN nodes outside the ATM network. The LES consists of three additional entities:

- LAN Emulation Server (LES)
- LAN Emulation Configuration Server (LECS)
- Broadcast and Unknown Server (BUS)

These three entities, along with the LAN Emulation Client (LEC), are discussed next.

Emulated LAN Components

Figure 11.4 gives a more detailed picture of the composition of an ELAN. We first define each of these components and then discuss how each component interacts with the others for LAN emulation.

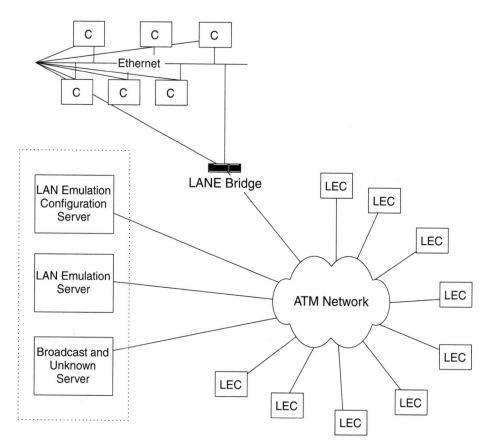

Figure 11.4   Emulated LAN components.

LAN Emulation Client (LEC)

Each station acting as an emulated LAN node uses a LAN Emulation Client (LE client). The LE client may be implemented as a piece of software or in a hardware add-in to the system. The LEC serves as the interface between the LANE end system and the ATM network. It forwards data to and from the network, and it provides an emulated Ethernet/ IEEE 802.3 or Token Ring/IEEE 802.5 MAC address for upper-layer network and application software. However, a LEC can emulate only one LAN type.

A LE client, by itself, can not form an emulated LAN, unless there is a mechanism through which it can interface with other LE clients. This function is served by the LAN Emulation Server (LE server).

LAN Emulation Server (LES)

The LAN Emulation Server (LES or LE server) provides a mechanism that allows LE clients to interact with each other. An LE client must register its emulated MAC address, multicast groups it wishes to join, and other reachability information with the LE server. The LE server facilitates address resolution for the ELAN and mediates interaction with other ELAN nodes by doing address and ATM route resolution.

Each ELAN has only one LE server, and each LE client is connected to only one LE server. However, since an end system can belong to more than one ELAN, this means that the system can have multiple instances of the LE client active at any time, each one connected to its own LE server.

LAN Emulation Configuration Server (LECS)

Before an LE client can hook up with an LE server to register its emulated MAC address, the LE client has to know which ELAN it belongs to and which LE server it should be talking to. The LAN Emulation Configuration Server (LECS) provides this service.

There must be at least one LECS in a LANE environment. Although there can be more that one, there is usually only one per administrative domain, serving all ELANs within that domain. The LECS assigns LE clients to LE servers based on preconfigured network policies, its own configuration database, and the information provided by the LE clients themselves and by other network devices. Assignment to a particular

ELAN may be made on the basis of the LE client's own geographic location (determined by the ATM address provided by the client) or by a destination LAN specified by the LE client.

All LE clients must be capable of using the configuration protocol to connect to an LECS and retrieve configuration information from the LECS. The LECS response to a request for configuration is an ATM address for the LE server associated with the LE client's assigned ELAN.

Broadcast and Unknown Server (BUS)

The Broadcast and Unknown Server (BUS) provides several important functions. First, it handles all data sent by LE clients to the broadcast MAC address (the "all-ones" address). The BUS distributes such broadcast data to other LE clients on the emulated LAN. The BUS also handles multicast traffic, distributing multicast frames to all multicast group members. Finally, the BUS handles "unknown" data—the initial unicasts that an LE client sends before a direct VCC has been set up for that client.

LANE Operation

It is not enough to map out the pieces of an emulated LAN. You've got to have connections between LE clients, LE servers, LECSs, and BUSs. The LAN Emulation Over ATM Version 2—LUNI Specification defines a set of different LAN emulation connections to carry flows. A LANE flow is carried over a Virtual Channel Connection (VCC) that can be point-to-point or point-to-multipoint. The VCC may be multiplexed to carry more than one flow. A flow contains the data and/or control traffic specific to a particular ELAN.

Those flows are carried over a variety of different connections, depending on who is sending the data, what kind of data they are sending, and to whom they are sending it. Flows are carried over VCCs that are related to the LANE functions for which they are being used. LANE functions depend on different types of VCC. In this section, we first look at the LANE functions themselves and then look at the different types of connections used for LANE.

LANE Functions

There are five steps to initializing a LANE connection. The first step, the Initial State, is basically just a starting point. At the initial state, the LE client and LE server have been given their basic starting configurations.

This includes basic parameters such as ATM and MAC addresses, the name of the ELAN to which they are (or are to be) connected, etc. Assuming a start at the initial state, the steps taken when initializing a LANE connection are as follows:

LECS Connect Phase. This is the first active part of the initialization, where the LE client establishes a connection with the LE Configuration Server with the intention of getting configured to actively participate in the ELAN.

Configuration Phase. During this phase, the LE client is directed to the LE Service for its ELAN. LE clients get configuration information from the LECS to be directed to LE services.

Join Phase. In this part of the initialization process, the LE client sets up control connections with its LE server. If the join procedure is successful, the client is assigned a unique LE Client identifier (LECID) and is notified of the unique identifier for the emulated LAN (ELAN_ID), maximum frame size, and emulated LAN type (Ethernet or Token Ring). Also, a control VCC will have been initiated between the LE client and the LE server. The LE client is now a part of the ELAN and has registered its own MAC address with the ELAN. If the Join procedure fails, the initialization process can begin again from the initial state.

Initial Registration. Once the LE client has joined the ELAN, it can register unicast and multicast LAN destinations and route descriptors in addition to the single unicast address that it registered as part of its join.

Connecting to the BUS. The last thing to do is to establish a connection to the Broadcast and Unknown Server (BUS). The LE client uses ARP for the layer 2 broadcast address (all zeroes). The response to this ARP points the LE client to the BUS. The LE client can set up a VCC for sending multicast data to the BUS, while the BUS sets up appropriate connections on which the LE client can receive multicasts.

Once all these steps are taken, the LE client can use the various servers to send and receive data as if it is connected to a LAN. When the LE client is ready to leave the network, it simply takes down all its VCCs to all the ELAN servers. When the connections are severed, the servers update their switching tables and don't bother attempting to deliver any data to that client. This is directly analogous to the way a real LAN works: When a host connected to an Ethernet LAN is turned off, any data sent to that node can be transmitted on the Ethernet, but all of the connected nodes ignore the transmissions. The LAN emulation service must do the same for data intended for a system that is not connected—it must not attempt to resurrect connections to a host that has terminated those connections.

LANE Connections

The LE client, LE server, LE configuration server, and BUS all must communicate over ATM VCCs. There are a number of different types of VCCs defined for this purpose. They may be bidirectional (meaning that there are actually two connections, one in each direction) or unidirectional (one direction only). They may be point-to-point or point-to-multipoint. They include the following:

Configuration Direct VCC. This is a bidirectional, point-to-point VCC set up by an LE client during the LECS connect phase. This connection is used to request and receive configuration information from the LECS.

Control Direct VCC. This is a bidirectional, point-to-point VCC set up by the LE client to the LE server during the initialization phase. The client uses this connection to register with the LE server. The connection is also used by the LE server to send control messages to the LE client, which must accept these messages and must also maintain this connection as long as the client is participating in the ELAN.

Control Distribute VCC. This is an optional unidirectional point-to-multipoint connection set up by the LE server during the initialization phase. This connection is used to distribute control information to all connected LE clients. If it is set up, it must remain up as long as the client and server are both connected to the ELAN.

Data Direct VCC. This is a bidirectional point-to-point connection linking LE clients, for the purpose of exchanging unicast traffic. A client that needs to send an ELAN frame to another client can determine the destination's ATM address through ARP and then set up the connection with the destination client.

Multicast Send VCCs. This is a bidirectional point-to-point connection, used by an LE client to send multicasts to the BUS. The connection is created after the client sends out an ARP request on the multicast (or broadcast) address. The BUS responds because it acts on behalf of the recipients of broadcasts and multicasts, and the client can create the VCC linking it to the BUS. An LE client must maintain at least one such connection for broadcasts as long as it is connected to the ELAN.

Multicast Forward VCCs. This is a unidirectional point-to-multipoint connection created and used by the BUS after a client has set up a multicast send VCC. The Multicast Forward VCC is used to distribute multicasts and broadcasts to clients set up to receive those transmissions.

IP over LANE

In theory, nothing special would have to happen to allow IP to work over LANE—at least not any more than would happen when IP runs over Ethernet or Token Ring or any other LAN type. Because LANE creates a network interface that looks like any other network interface, at least to a protocol stack, IP happily functions. However, the same old problem we encountered with IPOA—IP routing versus ATM switching—comes up with LANE. The ATM Forum created the Multi-Protocol over ATM (MPOA) protocol to help.

Multi-Protocol over ATM (MPOA)

As we saw in Chapter 10 and is shown in greater detail in Chapter 12, mapping an IP internetwork on top of an ATM internetwork does not always provide the most efficient mechanism for getting data from one place to another. When several different IP subnets are mapped onto an ATM network cloud, it means that packets passing from one subnet to another must be routed at layer 3 by an IP router, even if there is a direct path through the ATM cloud between the source and destination nodes.

Whether you map IP onto ATM, as described in Chapter 10, or do it by turning the ATM cloud into one or more emulated LANs, handling higher-layer protocol routing is still going to require a layer 3 router. That is unless you can use the Next Hop Resolution Protocol (NHRP) to build shortcuts through the ATM cloud. Even with NHRP and LANE together, there is still a problem with integrating IP (and other types of) internetworks on top of ATM: You can use NHRP when the shortcut is between the IP source and destination nodes, but it does not help when the destination node is not attached to the ATM network but is instead outside the ATM cloud.

The ATM Forum created the Multi-Protocol over ATM (MPOA) spec-ification to use both routing and bridging information to determine where its higher-layer packet can best leave the ATM cloud. Instead of deploying more routers, MPOA makes it possible for edge devices to behave sort of like routers but without the router overhead and without putting routers in the data path, which slows down traffic.

MPOA requires that LANE, NHRP, and standard ATM signaling pro-tocols be supported as prerequisites to supporting MPOA. It defines two types of devices—the MPOA Client (MPC) and the MPOA Server (MPS)—as well as the protocols necessary for these two types of devices to communicate.

An MPC is intended to serve as the anchor for internetwork short-cuts. It can act as the starting or ending point for these shortcuts. The MPC can do forwarding across the internetwork layer, but it doesn't run internetwork layer routing protocols itself. The MPS is incorpo-rated into a router that does do internetwork layer forwarding; the MPS provides forwarding information to the MPC.

The MPC can be notified when an MPS router is processing packets forwarded over an ELAN. When the MPC determines that the packet flow could be processed more efficiently through a shortcut, the MPC uses NHRP mechanisms to establish that shortcut. The MPC can also accept internetwork data from other MPCs for local forwarding. The MPC actually provides MPOA services to LE clients and can be served in turn by more than one MPS.

Reading List

There are currently no RFCs specifically addressing LANE and MPOA, though there are plenty of references to LANE and MPOA in RFCs and Internet-Drafts. You can download the full text of ATM forum specifica-tions from the ATM Forum's own ftp server. Other formats (Rich Text Format, Microsoft Word, and PostScript) are available on the ATM Forum Web site:

```
ftp://ftp.atmforum.com/pub/approved-specs/
```

Table 11.1 lists the ATM Forum specifications for LANE and MPOA, along with URLs for Portable Document Format (.pdf) versions of the documents.

Table 11.1 ATM Forum LANE and MPOA Specifications

DOCUMENT TITLE	URL
LAN Emulation over ATM 1.0	ftp://ftp.atmforum.com/pub/approved-specs/af-lane-0021.000.pdf
LAN Emulation Client Management Specification Version 1.0	ftp://ftp.atmforum.com/pub/approved-specs/af-lane-0038.000.pdf
LANE Servers Management Spec v1.0	ftp://ftp.atmforum.com/pub/approved-specs/af-lane-0050.000.pdf
LANE Servers Management Spec v1.0	ftp://ftp.atmforum.com/pub/approved-specs/af-lane-0057.000.pdf
LANE v2.0 LUNI Interface	ftp://ftp.atmforum.com/pub/approved-specs/af-lane-0084.000.pdf
Multi-Protocol over ATM Version 1	ftp://ftp.atmforum.com/pub/approved-specs/af-mpoa-0087.000.pdf
Multi-Protocol over ATM Version 1.0 MIB	ftp://ftp.atmforum.com/pub/approved-specs/af-mpoa-0092.000.pdf
LAN Emulation Client Management Specification Version 2.0	ftp://ftp.atmforum.com/pub/approved-specs/af-lane-0093.000.pdf
LAN Emulation over ATM Version 2	ftp://ftp.atmforum.com/pub/approved-specs/af-lane-0112.000.pdf
Multi-Protocol over ATM Version 1.1	ftp://ftp.atmforum.com/pub/approved-specs/af-mpoa-0114.000.pdf

CHAPTER

12

IP Routing through ATM

One of the problems with running IP over ATM is that both internet-working technologies use their own strategies for getting data from point A to point B. IP uses layer 3 routing, while ATM uses layer 2 switching. The IP network may or may not be exactly congruous with the ATM network. Sometimes ATM switching provides the most efficient path from source to destination, sometimes IP routing proves the better choice.

One important strategy for maximizing efficient network deliveries is embodied in the Next Hop Resolution Protocol (NHRP), a proposed Internet standard used in nonbroadcast multiple access (NBMA) networks including ATM. When an IP network architecture is laid over an ATM network cloud, it is sometimes more efficient to skip over IP routes and to use direct ATM connections between nodes. NHRP defines a strategy for determining how to create these shortcuts.

Another strategy for internetwork data delivery is embodied in the Multiprotocol Label Switching (MPLS) specifications developed in the MPLS working group of the IETF. Much similar work has been done by a number of network vendors, embodied in protected terms like "IP switching," "tag switching," and others. The basic objective of

157

these efforts is to map layer 3 routing onto layer 2 switching. The work-group has done a great deal of work starting early in 1997, but as of mid 1999, none of its drafts has been published as RFCs, and many of its drafts have not been updated since 1998. Much of the early vendor enthusiasm for similar proprietary solutions has waned; however, work continues.

In this chapter, we begin by looking at NHRP, discussing how it works and how it integrates with ATM networks. We conclude with a brief discussion of MPLS, how it works, and what its prospects are.

Creating Routing Complexity

As we've already seen, superimposing IP networks on top of ATM networks can create unwanted complexity. Figure 12.1 shows an ATM network cloud and several systems attached to that cloud. The black arrows indicate the actual movement of a packet from the source end station to the destination end station. The white arrow (piercing the ATM cloud) indicates the ideal path for data between those two end stations.

Why is the path so complex? Why does data have to be passed along three routers, even though all of the devices are connected to the same ATM cloud? The answer is straightforward, though perhaps not simple.

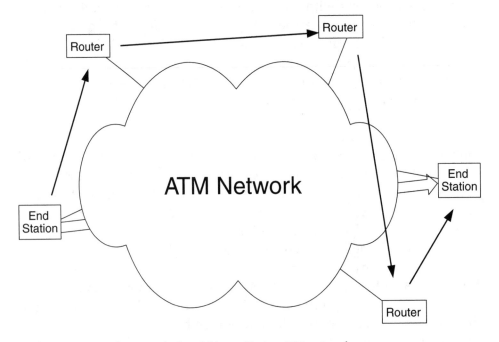

Figure 12.1   Routing complexity within an IP over ATM network.

Classical IP over ATM (RFC 2225) explicitly specifies that direct ATM connections can be used to transmit data only between nodes that are on the same logical IP subnet (LIS). If two or more subnets are mapped into a single ATM cloud, then packets passing from one LIS to another must be routed. Figure 12.2 shows the IP subnet architecture lying beneath the ATM cloud shown in Figure 12.1.

Because several IP hops are between the source and the destination, packets must be routed across three different routers. This is both inconvenient and a waste of resources. Each router hop costs in terms of resources (VCCs used) and in performance. Every layer 3 (IP) hop a packet takes across an ATM network means that the AAL5 frame has to be sliced up into ATM cells, transmitted, reassembled, passed up to the IP layer of the protocol stack, processed as a routed packet, repackaged into an AAL5 frame, resliced into new ATM cells, retransmitted, and so on.

Because ATM is not just another LAN technology but can incorporate many organizational and geographic entities, there may be quite a few LISs in any given ATM network cloud. The more LISs there are, the more likely it is that packets need to use suboptimal routes to cross the ATM cloud.

Another problem is illustrated in Figure 12.3. In this example, the destination node is not on the ATM network, but IP packets still have to bounce around that cloud before they make it to an exit router that can

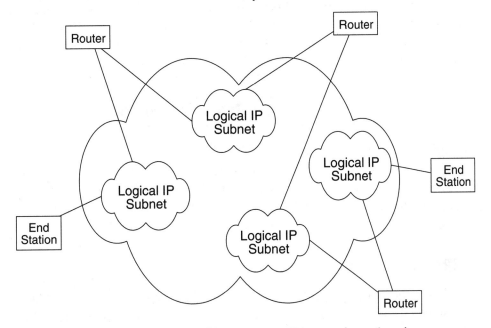

Figure 12.2   Routing complexity within an IP over ATM network, continued.

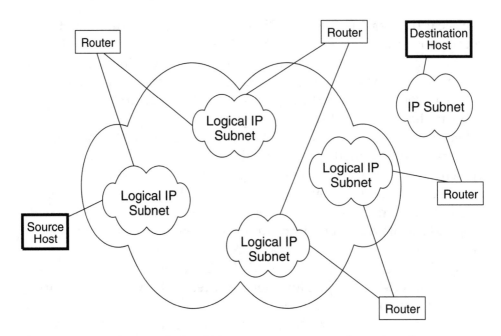

Figure 12.3   Routing complexity within an IP over ATM network, continued.

reach the destination node. Again, this is a scenario that is played out with increasing frequency as more IP networks are migrated to ATM.

If only there were a way to create a shortcut through the ATM network between the source and destination nodes or at least between the source node and an exit router. Of course, as has been mentioned elsewhere, there is a mechanism that makes this possible: the Next Hop Resolution Protocol (NHRP).

The Next Hop Resolution Protocol (NHRP)

In this section, we first introduce the Next Hop Resolution Protocol (NHRP) and discuss what it is, what it does, and where it came from. Then, we take a look at the protocol itself, discussing how it works. After a brief look at the NHRP protocol packet formats, we discuss how NHRP can be applied to networks in general and to ATM networks in particular.

NHRP Foundations

The proposed standard RFC 2332, "NBMA Next Hop Resolution Protocol (NHRP)" states: "The NBMA Next Hop Resolution Protocol (NHRP) allows a source station (a host or router), wishing to communicate over a Non-Broadcast, Multi-Access (NBMA) subnetwork, to determine the internetworking layer addresses and NBMA addresses of suitable 'NBMA next hops' toward a destination station." In other words, with NHRP you can figure out what the next hop should be according to the NBMA network (which is probably the shortcut) rather than what the next hop should be according to the IP network.

The purpose of NHRP is to help define these shortcuts through NBMA networks (such as ATM) to avoid packets being bounced around an NBMA network cloud by IP routers. With NHRP, nodes can determine what the best next hop is. If the destination node is attached to the same NBMA network as the sending node, then the best next hop is directly to the destination node. If the destination node is attached to a network outside the NBMA network, the best next hop is the edge router closest to the destination node. This router is called an "egress router" because it is the router through which the packet exits the NBMA network.

So far, the model for mapping IP over an NBMA network (for example, ATM) is to use the logical IP subnet (LIS) as a unit for routing. RFC 2332 refers to these as "logically independent IP subnets." An LIS has the following properties, according to RFC 2332:

- Every node belonging to the LIS has the same IP network number, IP subnet number, and the same subnet address mask.

- Every node belonging to the LIS is connected to the same NBMA subnetwork. In other words, you can have more than one LIS on a single ATM switch, but you can't have a single LIS spread out among more than one switch.

- All connectivity with nodes (hosts and routers) outside the LIS is mediated through a router. This includes connectivity with other nodes connected to the same NBMA network but on different IP subnets.

- Any node on an LIS can access any other node on the same LIS without having to go through a router.

ARP works only on the local link, but on an Ethernet that's enough. With ATMARP address resolution works only for nodes on the same LIS. Relying on ATMARP to determine the next hop won't give you the best next hop if more than one LIS is attached to the same ATM network cloud and the destination is connected to one of those. Instead, you'll just get connected to the router for the LIS to which the source node is attached.

A different approach to thinking about NBMA networks is to use the concept of a Local Address Group (LAG). In the LIS model, forwarding decisions are based entirely on the addressing information available to the entity deciding what to do with a packet. In other words, if a packet's IP address indicates its destination is on a different IP subnet, then the packet is forwarded to a router. The LAG approach is used to separate routing decisions from the address and use instead Quality of Service (QoS) and/or traffic characteristics to determine where the next hop should be. To achieve that kind of route decision making, some mechanism must exist on the NBMA router to resolve any network layer (IP) network address to a connected NBMA network address—without regard to whether the IP address of the destination is on the same IP subnet as the sender.

When such a mechanism like NHRP is in place, nodes can determine shortcuts through NBMA networks that bypass any internal routing through IP subnets located within the NBMA network. With the short-cut—the best next hop—a node can open an ATM circuit with the next hop station bypassing any superfluous IP routing. NHRP does not have to replace ATMARP (or other flavors of ARP adapted for a particular NBMA network), but it can coexist with ATMARP where there are nodes that can not use NHRP.

For a discussion of how NHRP works for NBMA networks in general, and particularly for a better understanding of why NHRP is valuable, read proposed standard RFC 2333, "NHRP Protocol Applicability Statement."

NBMA ADDRESS RESOLUTION PROTOCOL

In 1994, "NBMA Address Resolution Protocol (NARP)" was published as experimental RFC 1735. NARP provides a basic service: It allows a source node to determine the NBMA address of a destination node. It does so by putting one or more NBMA ARP Servers (NASs) on each NBMA network (more than one of which may make up an NBMA cloud). Each NAS keeps track of its own set of nodes as well as its peers elsewhere in the network.

A node sending a packet outside of its own subnet simply sends an NARP request to its NAS. The NAS either has direct knowledge of the destination, in which case it passes the destination address back to the requesting node or looks up which NAS *does* know about the destination address and relays the query to that NAS.

NARP is relevant to NHRP because it provides a basic service that is included as part of NHRP. Much of the language describing NARP has carried over into the NHRP specifications.

NHRP Protocol Overview

In NHRP, two different entities are defined: the Next Hop Server (NHS) and the Next Hop Client (NHC). An NHS is an entity that performs the NHRP service for entities inside an NBMA network. An NHC is any entity that initiates a request for NHRP services.

NOTE Clients get address resolution information from servers only; the source requests address resolution from the next hop server that serves the destination address, not from the destination itself. The response comes directly from the next hop server, which has gathered address resolution data from the destination (and other) nodes through a separate process. Finally, a next hop server can provide information about a node that isn't necessarily a next hop client (for example , is connected to an external network served by a router).

Put briefly, NHRP allows a source, either a router or a host, to determine the "NBMA next hop" to a destination. In other words, the source end station shown in Figures 12.1 and 12.2 can use NHRP to figure out the direct link to the destination end station instead of having its packets get passed from one router to another. Perhaps even better, with NHRP you can figure out a connection not only across logical IP subnets but also across logical NBMA subnetworks. This means that you can figure out shortcuts across entire ATM internetworks, not just across a single ATM switch.

NHRP works like this: On each NBMA subnetwork there is at least one Next Hop Server (NHS). The NHS is any entity that implements NHRP and can respond to an NHRP Resolution Request. Every NHS keeps a cache, storing NBMA subnet layer address resolution information, very much like a regular ARP server. As end stations use NHRP commands to register themselves with the NHS or to request information about other end stations, the NHS builds up its cache or the cache might be entered by hand (or some other mechanism).

An NHS may also be a router or similar entity, and it may also act as a regular ARP server. However, every NHS provides services to a group of specified destinations, and NHSs within an NBMA subnet cooperate to resolve best next hops.

By the process of elimination, any station that doesn't do NHS itself has to use an NHS to provide authoritative address resolution services for it. These types of end stations are referred to as NHRP Client or Next Hop Clients (NHCs). NHCs maintain their own caches, containing the responses they've received from NHSs. They may also include address mappings from other sources (perhaps from manual configuration or some other mechanism outside the scope of the protocol specification).

Figure 12.4 shows how it works. It all begins when the source host (which may be a host or a router) determines for some reason (usually because it wants to forward a routed or send a packet) that it needs to know the best next hop to that destination. The source can be either an end-user host or a router. The reason it wants to reach the destination is usually either to forward a packet or just because it wants to communicate with that destination. However, any type of communication between source and destination can trigger an NHRP request, including routing protocol updates.

The first thing the source node does is to figure out what the next network layer protocol hop is. In other words, it checks its IP routing logic and may determine that the destination is not on the same logical IP subnet and therefore must be sent to the default router. The next step is for the NHC to check its cache to see whether it already has an address mapping for that destination. If it does, then it's off to the races and sets up a circuit (in an ATM network) to the destination node.

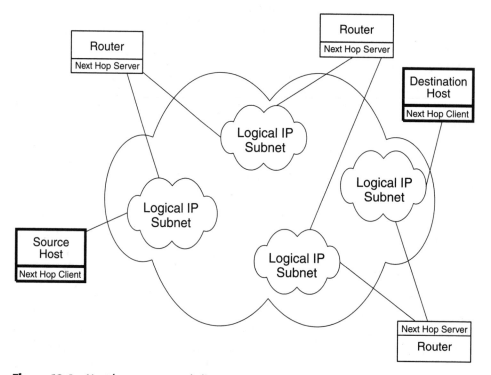

Figure 12.4 Next hop servers and clients.

PARTICIPATING IN NHRP

According to RFC 2332, an NHS is always "tightly coupled with a routing entity (router, route server or edge device)." This means that an NHS is likely to be implemented on the same device that does routing. It does not necessarily mean that any device that does routing is always an NHS. Furthermore, a router that does not also provide NHRP services can partition an NBMA network as far as NHRP is concerned. Figure 12.5 shows what happens: The LIS in the middle of the path does not have an NHS, thus the destination host is cut off.

If the client doesn't have a mapping for the destination, and the next hop (based on IP routing) is on an NBMA network link, the client can use NHRP. The first step is to generate an NHRP Resolution Request packet. Similar to the standard ARP packet, the NHRP Resolution Request packet contains the IP address (or, if not IP, whatever the network layer protocol address is) for both the source and the destination nodes as well as the NBMA network addressing information for the source node. RFC 2332 states that the sender now "emits the NHRP Resolution Request packet towards the destination." In other words, the client sends the request to its next hop server.

While it waits for a response to the NHRP request, the sending node can choose to drop the packet, hold onto the packet and wait for the best

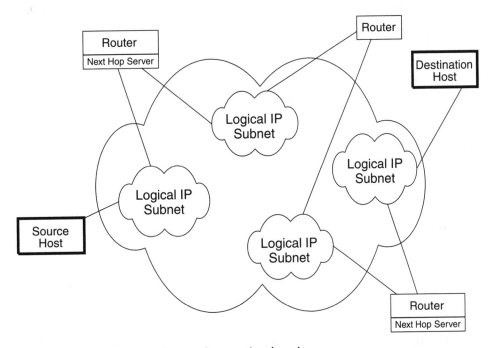

Figure 12.5 Fragmenting the next hop service domain.

next hop before sending it out, or just send the packet along the path indicated by the network layer protocol (IP). Any of these responses is OK, but the default is to use the routed path. This makes sense, since it means there is no disruption in the transmission of the packet even if it is not being sent by the best path.

When an NHS gets a resolution request, it checks to see whether the destination is one that the NHS serves directly. If the NHS does serve that destination, then it sends back a Resolution Reply indicating the NBMA address of the destination. When the actual NHS that serves the destination replies, the reply is considered "authoritative" and is so marked. A client can specify in the original request that only an authoritative reply will be accepted.

If the NHS does not serve the destination, it forwards the request to the next NHS. It may determine the *next* next hop server with a variety of mechanisms, which we mention in the next section. In any case, the next NHS checks to see if it serves the destination and, if not, passes the request on to the next NHS. This continues until it is either determined that the destination is not reachable or the destination does not have a mapping on the NBMA network. In that case, a negative response is generated. Otherwise, an authoritative reply is generated (as described above) and forwarded to the source.

Intermediate next hop servers are permitted to cache the address resolution information that they relay from other servers. A nonauthoritative reply occurs when an NHS responds to a request with address resolution information that is taken from such a cache. The purpose for distinguishing authoritative from nonauthoritative replies is to provide a tool for troubleshooting. When a source node first uses a nonauthoritative address resolution and fails to get through to the destination, it can try again but this time insist on an authoritative address. Cached addresses can get stale and not reflect the current state of the network, so a destination should not be considered unreachable if the destination's address has been acquired second-hand from a transit server's cache rather than from the NHS actually serving the destination.

When the destination address is outside the NBMA network, the destination can still be served by an NHS. In that case, the NHS sends back the NBMA address of the edge router that should be used to exit the NBMA network. Figure 12.6 shows the architecture. Under NHRP, routing information (a prefix length) can also be returned with this information. The prefix length, along with the destination address, can be used to indicate what range of network addresses would normally be served

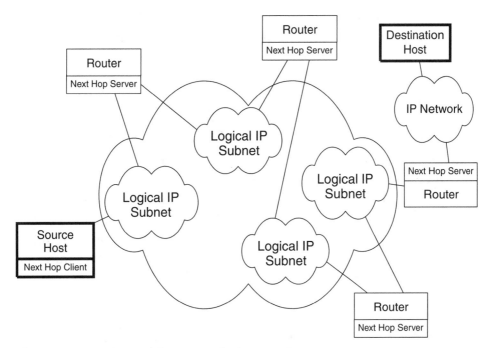

Figure 12.6 Getting an exit router as the best next hop.

by the same exit router. The best next hop in Figure 12.6 is to the edge router shown connected to both the NBMA network cloud and the IP network. That NHS can send, along with its reply to a resolution request, information about the range of IP addresses it serves in that outer IP network, which may be the entire Internet, for example.

NHRP Packets

There are seven basic NHRP packet types:

Resolution Request. This is the packet that an NHC sends out when it needs to resolve an address and get the best next hop. It performs a similar function as an ARP request in non-NBMA networks.

SERVER CACHE SYNCHRONIZATION

Next hop servers are closely associated with devices that can do routing. Groups of these servers need some mechanism to keep track of nodes and logical IP subnets. RFC 2334, "Server Cache Synchronization Protocol (SCSP)," provides such a mechanism. This proposed standard specifies a protocol that uses an algorithm similar to that used by OSPF for synchronizing server caches. Another proposed standard, RFC 2335, "A Distributed NHRP Service Using SCSP," defines how such a service can be used with the NHRP.

Resolution Reply. This is the packet that an NHS sends out in response to a resolution request. It performs a similar function as an ARP response in non-NBMA networks.

Registration Request. This is a packet sent out to notify the NHS of the station's NBMA address information. It is sent out when the station becomes available on the network, and the information in it is used by the NHS to build its address resolution cache.

Registration Reply. This is the reply sent out by the NHS in reply to an end station's Registration Request. The reply indicates whether the Registration Request was successful, with an acknowledgment (ACK), or unsuccessful, with a negative acknowledgment (NAK).

Purge Request. Either an NHC or an NHS can send a purge request. A server sends a purge request when address resolution information that it previously sent to a client is no longer valid. A client can send a purge request when it wishes to have its address resolution removed before it would otherwise expire. A station receiving a Purge Request must remove from its cache any entry that matches the request.

Purge Reply. This must be sent any time a station receives a purge request, even if the purge request does not match any cache entries at the receiving station.

Error Indication. This packet is sent when a station receives an NHRP packet that causes any type of error. The error indication packet notifies the sender that the error exists and provides an error code.

Each protocol packet consists of three different parts: fixed, mandatory, and extensions. The fixed part is always 20 bytes long and is present in all NHRP packets. The mandatory part must be present in all NHRP packets, but its length and contents vary depending on which type of packet it is. The extensions part also varies depending on the type of packet and is not always present. These are each discussed in the sections below.

NHRP packets are not encapsulated within IP or any other network layer protocol, but are packaged at the NBMA network layer. Thus, when running over ATM, an NHRP packet is either encapsulated by an LLC/SNAP header in a multiprotocol network or not encapsulated when only one network protocol is in use (as per RFC 1483).

Fixed Part

Every NHRP packet includes a 20-byte fixed part. Figure 12.7, taken from RFC 2332, shows the fields in this part of the NHRP packet. The

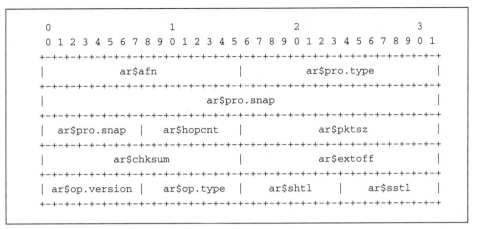

Figure 12.7 The NHRP packet fixed part (from RFC 2332).

list of header field definitions, also taken from RFC 2332, follows in Table 12.1. In a nutshell, the fixed part contains information about the network and the NHRP packet itself.

Table 12.1 NHRP Packet Fixed Part Header Fields (Adapted from RFC 2332)

NAME	DESCRIPTION
ar$afn	Defines the type of link layer addresses being carried. This number is taken from the address family number list specified in STD 2, Assigned Numbers.
ar$pro.type	A 16-bit unsigned integer indicating what type of protocol is in use. Includes protocols defined by or used by ATM Forum, ethertypes, or Network Layer Protocol IDs; used for experimental/local use or reserved for future use by the IETF.
ar$pro.snap	When the ar$pro.type field has a value of 0x0080, it indicates that a SNAP encoded extension is being used to encode the protocol type. In that case, the SNAP extension is place in the ar$pro.snap field. In all other cases (ar$pro.type has a value of anything BUT 0x0080), this field must be set to zero and ignored on receive.
ar$hopcnt	The hop count indicates the maximum number of NHSs that an NHRP packet is allowed to traverse before being discarded. This hop count field works in much the same way as the IP Time to Live (TTL) field.
ar$pktsz	The total length of the NHRP packet, in octets (excluding link layer encapsulation).

Continues

Table 12.1 NHRP Packet Fixed Part Header Fields (Adapted from RFC 2332) *(Continued)*

NAME	DESCRIPTION
ar$chksum	The standard IP checksum over the entire NHRP packet starting at the fixed header.
ar$extoff	This field identifies the existence and location of NHRP extensions. If this field is 0 then no extensions exist, otherwise this field represents the offset from the beginning of the NHRP packet (that is, starting from the ar$afn field) of the first extension.
ar$op.version	This field indicates what version of generic address mapping and management protocol is represented by this message. A 0 indicates the MARS protocol, a 1 indicates NHRP as defined in RFC 2332. All other values are reserved the IETF, allocated to the ATM Forum. The value 0xFF is assigned for experimental/local uses.
ar$op.type	When the ar$op.version indicates NHRP (is equal to 1), then this field is used to specify packet type (1 for resolution request, 2 for resolution reply, 3 for registration request, 4 for registration reply, 5 for purge request, 6 for purge reply, and 7 for error indication).
ar$shtl	Type and length of source NBMA address interpreted in the context of the address family number indicated by ar$afn.
ar$sstl	Type and length of source NBMA subaddress (NSAP, for example) interpreted in the context of the address family number indicated by ar$afn.

Mandatory Part

Though every NHRP packet has to have both a fixed part and a mandatory part, the fixed part will look the same for all packets while the mandatory part varies because it contains a common header plus optional Client Information Entries (CIEs), which may contain data of different lengths depending on the type of NBMA network in use. Thus, the mandatory part may consist of nothing more than the common header, or it may contain one or more CIEs.

All the NHRP packet types except the error indication have only slightly different formats and headers. The error indication is unique in that it will not include a CIE. In this section, we summarize the basic features common to the other six NHRP packet types, but refer the reader to RFC 2332 for all the details of the different packet type fields. Figure 12.8, taken from RFC 2332, shows the common part, while Figure 12.9, also from RFC 2332, shows the Client Information Entry (CIE) format.

```
 0                   1                   2                   3
 0 1 2 3 4 5 6 7 8 9 0 1 2 3 4 5 6 7 8 9 0 1 2 3 4 5 6 7 8 9 0 1
+-+-+-+-+-+-+-+-+-+-+-+-+-+-+-+-+-+-+-+-+-+-+-+-+-+-+-+-+-+-+-+-+
| Src Proto Len | Dst Proto Len |              Flags            |
+-+-+-+-+-+-+-+-+-+-+-+-+-+-+-+-+-+-+-+-+-+-+-+-+-+-+-+-+-+-+-+-+
|                           Request ID                          |
+-+-+-+-+-+-+-+-+-+-+-+-+-+-+-+-+-+-+-+-+-+-+-+-+-+-+-+-+-+-+-+-+
|               Source NBMA Address (variable length)           |
+-+-+-+-+-+-+-+-+-+-+-+-+-+-+-+-+-+-+-+-+-+-+-+-+-+-+-+-+-+-+-+-+
|             Source NBMA Subaddress (variable length)          |
+-+-+-+-+-+-+-+-+-+-+-+-+-+-+-+-+-+-+-+-+-+-+-+-+-+-+-+-+-+-+-+-+
|             Source Protocol Address (variable length)         |
+-+-+-+-+-+-+-+-+-+-+-+-+-+-+-+-+-+-+-+-+-+-+-+-+-+-+-+-+-+-+-+-+
|           Destination  Protocol Address (variable length)     |
+-+-+-+-+-+-+-+-+-+-+-+-+-+-+-+-+-+-+-+-+-+-+-+-+-+-+-+-+-+-+-+-+
```

Figure 12.8   The common fields of the NHRP mandatory part.

The fields in the common part include the following:

Src Proto Len is the length (in bytes) of the Source Protocol Address.

Dst Proto Len is the length (in bytes) of the Destination Protocol Address.

Flags are specific to each different message type and are defined for each in RFC 2332.

Request ID contains a value used with the address of the source to uniquely identify the information contained in a request packet. When a server replies to a request, it copies this value from the request packet. When the client gets a request reply back, it compares this value with any outstanding requests. If it matches, the sender knows that the original request has been responded to.

Source NBMA Address is the NBMA address of the source station sending the request. For ATM, this translates to the calling party address used when the station signals for an SVC.

Source NBMA SubAddress is the NBMA subaddress (NSAP address for ATM, for example) of the station sending the request. If the network in question does not support a subaddress, then the ar$sstl field in the Fixed Part is set to 0 and this field has a length of zero bytes.

Source Protocol Address is the network layer protocol (IP) address of the station sending the request. This is the address to which replies are sent.

Destination Protocol Address is the network layer protocol (IP) address of the station for which address resolution/best next hop is desired.

The Client Information Entry (CIE) occurs "zero or more" times in an NHRP packet. There might be one CIE in a Registration Request, while there might be zero in a Resolution Reply that was reporting no best next hops, or there might be more than one CIE in a Resolution Reply that is reporting more than one next hops that meet the request's criteria. The CIE format is shown in Figure 12.9. Descriptions of the header fields follow.

The fields in the CIE include the following:

Code contains some type of acknowledgment code for the particular message. In general, a 0 in the field indicates a positive ACK; other values indicate a NAK. Different values indicate different reasons for the negative acknowledgment.

Prefix Length depends on the packet type, but generally is used to indicate that the data in the message is relevant to a class of inter-network (IP) addresses instead of just one specific address. If this field contains 0x00 (or 0xFF), the field must be ignored. Any other value indicates the number of bits of the network (IP) layer address to use to specify the equivalence class. In other words, the value 0x08 here indicates that any IP address with the first 8 bits matching the address in the NHRP message can use the same next hop.

```
 0                   1                   2                   3
 0 1 2 3 4 5 6 7 8 9 0 1 2 3 4 5 6 7 8 9 0 1 2 3 4 5 6 7 8 9 0 1
+-+-+-+-+-+-+-+-+-+-+-+-+-+-+-+-+-+-+-+-+-+-+-+-+-+-+-+-+-+-+-+-+
|    Code       | Prefix Length |            unused             |
+-+-+-+-+-+-+-+-+-+-+-+-+-+-+-+-+-+-+-+-+-+-+-+-+-+-+-+-+-+-+-+-+
| Maximum Transmission Unit     |          Holding Time         |
+-+-+-+-+-+-+-+-+-+-+-+-+-+-+-+-+-+-+-+-+-+-+-+-+-+-+-+-+-+-+-+-+
| Cli Addr T/L | Cli SAddr T/L | Cli Proto Len |   Preference   |
+-+-+-+-+-+-+-+-+-+-+-+-+-+-+-+-+-+-+-+-+-+-+-+-+-+-+-+-+-+-+-+-+
|             Client NBMA Address (variable length)            |
+-+-+-+-+-+-+-+-+-+-+-+-+-+-+-+-+-+-+-+-+-+-+-+-+-+-+-+-+-+-+-+-+
|           Client NBMA Subaddress (variable length)           |
+-+-+-+-+-+-+-+-+-+-+-+-+-+-+-+-+-+-+-+-+-+-+-+-+-+-+-+-+-+-+-+-+
|           Client Protocol Address (variable length)          |
+-+-+-+-+-+-+-+-+-+-+-+-+-+-+-+-+-+-+-+-+-+-+-+-+-+-+-+-+-+-+-+-+
```

Figure 12.9 The Client Information Entry (CIE) fields of the NHRP mandatory part.

Maximum Transmission Unit indicates the maximum transmission unit (MTU) size for the relevant client station. A value of 0 indicates either that the default MTU is to be used or that the station will negotiate an MTU during the signaling process if that is permitted on the network.

Holding Time specifies, in seconds, how long the next hop information in the CIE can be considered valid. The next hop information is discarded when the holding time has passed.

Cli Addr T/L is the type and length of the next hop NBMA address specified in the CIE. The data in this field is treated as appropriate for the network type indicated in the ar$afn field of the fixed part.

Cli SAddr T/L is the type and length of the next hop NBMA subaddress specified in the CIE. Again, this depends on the context provided by the ar$afn field. For networks that don't use subaddresses, the value is null and the length is 0.

Cli Proto Len is the length, in bytes, of the client protocol address indicated in the CIE.

Preference specifies whether a specific CIE is to be given preference over some other CIE(s). A higher value here means that the CIE should be given preference. In the event of a tie, the decision is left to the local implementation.

Client NBMA Address is the client's NBMA address.

Client NBMA SubAddress is the client's NBMA subaddress.

Client Protocol Address is the client's network layer (IP) address.

Extensions Part

NHRP packet extensions behave much like any other Internet protocol extensions. The Extensions Part of the NHRP packet consists of three pieces: a type field to specify the type of extension, a length field to indicate how long the extension is, and a value field that contains the actual extension content.

Several extensions are defined in RFC 2332, including the following:

Responder Address Extension is used to determine the address of the entity that generates an appropriate reply for a particular request packet.

NHRP Forward Transit NHS Record Extension contains a list of the NHSs through which a request has been passed.

NHRP Reverse Transit NHS Record Extension contains a list of the NHSs through which a reply has been passed.

NHRP Authentication Extension is used for authentication of request and reply packets.

NHRP Vendor-Private Extension is used for carrying information relevant to extensions built into private vendor's implementations.

Applying NHRP to ATM

The informational RFC 2336, "Classical IP and ARP over ATM to NHRP Transition," describes how to gracefully shift from the classical IP over ATM (RFC 2225) approach to address resolution (ATMARP) to the NHRP approach. This RFC notes that not all clients will make the change from ATMARP to NHRP at the same time and that the two approaches will most likely need to be accommodated simultaneously within networks.

The mechanism suggested in RFC 2336 is to require NHSs to respond to ATMARP clients as if the NHS is an ATMARP server. NHRP servers and ATMARP servers are not permitted to coexist within a logical IP subnet. The NHS has to maintain ATMARP information that is distinct from NHRP information in its cache. The next hop server's response to an NHRP request will only be the same as its response to an ATMARP request if the destination station is on the same LIS as the requesting station. If the destination is on a separate LIS, the NHS must send a NAK when it receives an ATMARP request for that destination—even though it can resolve the destination with a best next hop that spans IP subnets.

Multiprotocol Label Switching (MPLS)

In 1996, the networking industry was buzzing with the newest hot technology. One company, Ipsilon (later acquired by Nokia) got the trademark name "IP switching." Other companies took what they could get as far as product names: Cisco staked out "tag switching," 3Com called it "FastIP," Ascend had something called "IP Navigator," and there were others. Basically, these were all layer 2 switching mechanisms that were particularly well adapted for use in ATM networks that spanned more than one IP subnet.

Cisco's tag switching, coupled with work done at Hitachi and IBM, turned into the IETF's Multiprotocol Label Switching (MPLS) effort. The MPLS working group has expended and continues to expend considerable effort toward specifying acceptable standards on label switching. As of mid 1999, the group has not had any of its Internet-Drafts approved for publication as RFCs. Titles of drafts available online include:

- A Framework for Multiprotocol Label Switching
- Use of Label Switching with RSVP
- Multiprotocol Label Switching Architecture
- MPLS Label Stack Encoding
- The Assignment of the Information Field and Protocol Identifier in the Q.2941 Generic Identifier and Q.2957 User-to-User Signaling for the Internet Protocol
- Use of Label Switching on Frame Relay Networks Specification
- VCID Notification over ATM link
- Carrying Label Information in BGP-4
- Requirements for Traffic Engineering over MPLS
- LDP Specification
- Definitions of Managed Objects for the Multiprotocol Label Switching, Label Distribution Protocol (LDP)
- MPLS Using ATM VC Switching
- LDP State Machine
- Extensions to RSVP for LSP Tunnels
- Constraint-Based LSP Setup Using LDP
- MPLS Traffic Engineering Management Information Base Using SMIv2
- MPLS Capability Set
- Explicit Tree Routing
- MPLS Support of Differentiated Services by ATM LSRs and Frame Relay LSRs
- MPLS Loop Prevention Mechanism
- Framework for IP Multicast in MPLS
- MPLS Label Switch Router Management Information Base Using SMIv2

For the most current versions of these drafts and for any new drafts, check the workgroup page at:

```
http://www.ietf.org/html.charters/mpls-charter.html
```

In this section, we provide a brief introduction to the concepts behind MPLS, based on a work in progress by members of the MPLS working group. Because none of the MPLS specifications have been published as RFCs, we can't really describe them as anything but works in progress. Significant changes are still possible and even likely.

Conventional IP Forwarding

IP packets (or the packets of any other connectionless network layer protocol) travel from one router to another on their way from source to destination. Each router that processes the packets must make its own independent decision about how to forward each packet. The router examines the packet headers, uses various algorithms to determine where the packet is going and how the router can forward the packet so it will advance in its path to its ultimate destination.

Strictly speaking, the only information really necessary to actually make the routing decision about any particular packet is the destination address. The IP header carries much more information relating to fragmentation, the header itself, and other fields that don't have any impact on which interface a router ultimately decides to forward the packet. The task of deciding what the packet's next IP hop is thus depends simply on what the destination address is and what options the router has regarding the next hop for the packet.

The task of the router, therefore, can be treated as two separate functions. First, there is the task of dividing packets up into groups called Forwarding Equivalence Classes (FECs). All members of an FEC are forwarded in the same way. Consider an edge router that connects an intranet, consisting of a single IP subnet, with the Internet. Any packet headed for the Internet from the intranet is a member of a single FEC; the next hop for any such packet is on the router's link with its Internet service provider. This is the essence of the second function: mapping a next hop to each FEC.

As far as the router is concerned, there is no difference in terms of how the packet is handled by the router between a packet headed for any point on the Internet—as long as all packets being forwarded to the Internet go out the same interface to the same next hop router.

Assigning IP packets to FECs is usually just a matter of comparing the routed packet's destination address with network prefixes in the router's routing table. If the address prefix (X bits long) matches the first X bits of the destination address, the packet belongs to that prefix's FEC. Every time the packet is received by a router, it must reclassify the packet based on its destination address and put it into an FEC. It then figures out what the next hop is and forwards the packet.

Label Switching and IP

So, what does this all have to do with ATM and label switching? A lot. As we've already seen, IPOA and MPOA treat logical IP subnets as separate entities through which packets are routed. Without NHRP, routed packets traveling through an ATM cloud can take quite a ride. Between the setting up of circuits between LIS routers and turning the IP packet into ATM cells and then back again as many times as it takes to reach the destination station, performance will suffer. Even with NHRP, a certain amount of overhead is required as the NHRP request and reply are generated. While waiting for the NHRP reply, packets are still routed as before from LIS to LIS through the ATM cloud.

Here's what Multiprotocol Label Switching (MPLS) brings to the table: As the packet enters the NBMA (ATM) network, it is assigned to an FEC. Once. As it enters the edge device, the packet gets assigned to an FEC based on its destination, and that FEC is encoded into a label: a short, fixed-length value that switching devices within the NBMA network is able to interpret. If you know which device put the label on the packet, you can look at that label and determine what the packet's next hop should be.

By assigning the packet to an FEC as it enters the NBMA network, such classification is not necessary at subsequent hops within the NBMA. Instead, forwarding devices maintain tables that list inbound labels along with a next hop and a new label to attach to the packet as it is forwarded. When the forwarding device receives a packet, it looks at the label and looks up that label on its routing table to see what the next hop for that packet should be. Then, it strips off the old label, replaces it with the label listed in the table, and forwards the packet on to the device indicated as the next hop in the routing table.

But what's all this about routing and packets? The protocol specification documents tend to speak of routers. A Label Switching Router (LSR) is a device that supports MPLS. Thus, an ATM switch can function perfectly happily as an LSR, and the labels can be encoded into the VCI/VPI header fields of an ATM cell, making it possible for MPLS to finesse the issue of doing address resolution through next hop resolution or ATMARP. All forwarding is preconfigured through the labels.

> **NOTE** MPLS is not specifically an ATM protocol, though it tends to work well with ATM and often is discussed in terms of deployment on ATM networks. Likewise, MPLS is often discussed in terms of IP, though it can just as easily be used for any other network layer protocol.

The other big questions are how do the LSRs know how to link a next hop with a particular label, and how do they know which labels they should use to replace incoming cells' labels with? LSRs use a label distribution protocol of some sort or another. The LSRs pass information about their labels to other LSRs within the network in a manner reminiscent of routers notifying other routers of their available links.

MPLS offers a number of advantages over more conventional mechanisms for routing packets. MPLS can be implemented on switches, which tend to be simpler and cheaper, rather than on routers, which need to be able to do more processing and can be more expensive.

For another, LSRs are not limited to using the network layer protocol header data when they assign a packet to an FEC with MPLS. An LSR might assign a packet to a different FEC depending on from which network interface it was received. Thus, an ISP might be able to forward packets from its better customers on a fast track while treating packets received from economy subscribers differently.

MPLS also permits the network to treat packets differently depending on where they enter the network—even if the packets are headed for the same destination. For example, if a packet comes into the network via the router serving a corporation's executive office, it might be given a less direct route than packets entering the network from the direct sales department. With plain IP, you could put a fatter pipe into networks that need them. However, once a packet is routed away from its local router it is treated just like any other packet. MPLS makes it possible for a packet to get special treatment across IP networks.

Another benefit to MPLS is that it keeps the routing logic in one place, at the edge where the packet is assigned to an FEC, without requiring any of the LSRs to be updated or upgraded. Those label-switching devices continue to pass switching information among themselves and just forward packets as they get them. The mechanisms by which incoming packets are assigned to FECs can be made more complicated without affecting the rest of the network.

Finally, MPLS makes it possible to optionally encode class of service (that is, Quality of Service) into labels. As we see in Chapter 13, this is a good potential solution to a sometimes thorny problem.

Reading List

Table 12.2 lists some of the RFCs relevant to the Next Hop Resolution Protocol. The interested reader should check out the MPLS working group home page (at www.ietf.org/html.charters/mpls-charter.html) for pointers to the most up-to-date Internet-Drafts (as well as to any newly published RFCs). See also the Web site for this series at:

```
http://www.Internet-Standard.com
```

Updates regarding changes in status of MPLS drafts and any updates to this chapter (or any other part of the series) are posted here.

Table 12.2   Next Hop Resolution Protocol RFCs

RFC	TITLE
RFC 1735	NBMA Address Resolution Protocol (NARP)
RFC 2332	NBMA Next Hop Resolution Protocol (NHRP)
RFC 2333	NHRP Protocol Applicability Statement
RFC 2334	Server Cache Synchronization Protocol (SCSP)
RFC 2335	A Distributed NHRP Service Using SCSP
RFC 2335	A Distributed NHRP Service Using SCSP
RFC 2336	Classical IP and ARP over ATM to NHRP Transition
RFC 2520	NHRP with Mobile NHCs
RFC 2583	Guidelines for Next Hop Client (NHC) Developers

Managing Network Traffic

To understand how ATM, quality of service, resource reservation, and IP all work together, it is helpful to track the development of the Integrated Service (IS) model, real-time services, and the Resource Reservation Protocol (RSVP) as they relate to ATM. In this chapter, we begin with a background discussion of these topics. Then, we take a look at the current IETF standards for resource reservation, real-time applications, quality of service, integrated services, and ATM.

Quality of Service (QoS) is one mechanism available for managing network traffic. Under IPv4, the Type of Service (ToS) field as originally (and vaguely) defined never served this purpose particularly well. The ToS field has been redefined as the Differentiated Services field in RFC 2474, "Definition of the Differentiated Services Field (DS Field) in the IPv4 and IPv6 Headers." However, ATM works hand in glove with the Integrated Services (IS) model, which is better designed for mapping IP QoS and resource reservations on top of ATM QoS and resource reservations.

Traffic Management Issues

On the average network, such as (oh, for instance) Ethernet, all traffic is created equal. One Ethernet frame is treated much like another. There is no way to flag a particular frame for special treatment, nor is there any way to flag another frame to indicate it's nothing particularly urgent. Frames are sent out, and frames are received. If one node tries to send a frame out at the same time another frame is in transit (remember, Ethernet is a broadcast medium), the node backs off for a little while and tries again. It doesn't matter whether the frame that was in transit just contained part of the latest Dilbert cartoon while the frame that got delayed was an urgent video transmission from the president of the company; it's (basically) first-come, first-served.

This is actually not so bad, as long as traffic doesn't become so congested that nothing gets through, and as long as the traffic is of the type common on IP networks for the first 20 or 25 years of its history. File-transfer oriented protocols, such as the File Transfer Protocol (FTP) and the Hypertext Transfer Protocol (HTTP), are forgiving of network delays and slow links. As long as the file eventually gets to its destination the network and the protocol are doing what they are supposed to do. Whether it takes 2 seconds or 20 seconds, the only difference is the happiness of the user with application response time. The same goes for terminal emulation-oriented protocols such as telnet and the r-utilities. Most of the terminal emulation exchanges are transmission of very brief commands from client to server and the transmission of updated (text-based) screens from server to client. Considering that it is possible to encapsulate most terminal data in one or two packets, lengthy delays in a moderately healthy network are unlikely.

In any case, occasional delays are the price to be paid for reliable transport via TCP and IP. If a flow of data from a terminal or file server is disrupted or corrupted beyond repair, it doesn't get completed, and it doesn't get completed until it has been completely and accurately communicated from node to node. Accuracy and completeness are provided at the expense of timeliness.

By the early 1990s, there was a great deal of talk about real-time applications with much different requirements. In particular, accuracy for certain types of applications is not as important as timeliness. Voice transmissions, for example, cannot be batch transmitted but need real-time transmission: The bits have to get there in the same order and at the same rate they were created. It's less important that all the bits get there, as long as most of them get to their destination in order. The person listening at the other end can fill in the gaps if there aren't too many of them; however, the person listening at the other end can't interpret the bits if they are delivered in the wrong order.

It's clear that this new type of real-time application places different requirements on internetwork transports than traditional network applications. With IP, typically routers had choices only about where to route a packet. There was no way you could tell routers along a path between two nodes that they need to reserve a certain amount of bandwidth to carry a videoconference. There was no way to notify routers that packets in a particular stream need to be delivered in a controlled stream that is neither too fast nor too slow. Furthermore, just because one packet got through in the right amount of time doesn't mean that the following packets in the stream would be as successful. Some mechanism for specifying how packets should be treated is necessary, as is some mechanism or mechanisms for controlling traffic as it passes through a network.

In this section, we introduce the basics of ATM network traffic control. Then, we look at different mechanisms that have been tried and proposed to differentiate network types of service.

ATM Traffic Control

You can have all the bandwidth in the world, but the actual rate at which data crosses a network is called throughput. Although throughput can theoretically have the same rate as the overall network bandwidth, in practice it is never that fast. Throughput can be limited by data loss, by implementation of the network protocols in the intermediate and end systems carrying the data, and by various network delays. Data loss on the link can be minimized by the use of flow control, in particular that implemented with the Transmission Control Protocol (TCP). However, network congestion—the state where there is too much traffic for the network transports and the intermediate systems to handle—can cause both traffic delays and traffic loss. Packets are merely delayed when the buffers of intermediate systems are able to hold onto the extra traffic while waiting for a break in the traffic. When the buffers overflow, packets are "dropped on the floor" or simply discarded.

TCP flow control mechanisms handle traffic variations remarkably well to ensure that a stream of data arrives at its destination while taking advantage of the available bandwidth through the TCP virtual circuit. However, TCP provides a reliable service, which means that every bit of data being sent is received. TCP does not provide any guarantees about timeliness—it may take half a minute or half a second, but the sender won't stop until it has determined the recipient is unreachable or until the recipient has acknowledged receipt of every bit of data.

Reliability is a useful feature for a data circuit, but it is not as useful for the newer type of real-time applications mentioned earlier. It certainly is not as useful as timeliness of delivery. Unfortunately, the TCP/IP suite was not originally designed with this objective in mind. Fortunately, ATM—as a telecommunications technology—was designed with the goal of providing real-time service.

The ATM Forum specifies four basic traffic classes for ATM data flows:

Constant Bit Rate (CBR). This is the class that most closely approximates a nonvirtual circuit (or a real wired connection between the endpoints). A peak cell rate (PCR) is the maximum rate at which the station can transmit. The PCR defines how much bandwidth should be assigned to a CBR data flow, and that bandwidth is roped off and allocated entirely to the CBR data flow. CBR is used for applications that require a constant amount of bandwidth such as real-time video or audio transmissions.

Variable Bit Rate (VBR). This traffic class is defined both by a PCR and by a Maximum Burst Size (MBS). The PCR in this case represents the maximum average rate at which the user can transmit. When necessary, the user can send more than the PCR (a burst) as long as the average bandwidth use remains at or below the PCR. VBR is useful for video and audio data that has been compressed. In these cases, the average amount of bandwidth needed can be calculated, but the actual transmissions over time vary depending on how much compression is done on the current bit stream (a compressed blue screen requires less bandwidth than a compressed action scene from "Gone With the Wind"). VBR comes in two flavors, real-time VBR (rt-VBR) and non-real-time VBR (nrt-VBR). The real-time version is more sensitive to cell delays and losses than the non-real-time version. Non-real-time VBR is appropriate for data applications such as transaction processing.

Unspecified Bit Rate (UBR). This is the equivalent of the IP best-effort delivery service with no guarantees. Applications that use the UBR service get their data sent out if there is bandwidth available; if no bandwidth is available, the bits don't get sent (they are usually buffered for sending later, when bandwidth becomes available). If the bandwidth never opens up, the data never gets sent. UBR traffic is characterized by a PCR (though this specifies only the upper limit on the total available bandwidth of the connection) and by something called a Cell Delay Variation Tolerance (CDVT). The CDVT indicates how long the application is willing or able to wait between receiving cells. UBR is appropriate for applications that are not at all sensitive to delays or that are only marginally sensitive to delays, for example, email, file transfers, terminal emulation, and other traditional Internet or network applications.

Available Bit Rate (ABR). This traffic class provides a minimum amount of bandwidth and at the same time allows more flexibility than is possible with VBR. ABR traffic is characterized by a PCR (again, as with UBR, the peak cell rate specifies the upper limit of the link) and by a Minimum Cell Rate (MCR), which defines the least amount of bandwidth that the application can accept (this value can actually be set to zero, if it makes sense for the application). ABR is appropriate for applications that are more sensitive to cell loss than they are to cell delay.

Thus, in addition to traffic classes, ATM services are differentiated on the basis of required bandwidth, tolerance for cell delays, average cell rates, minimum required bandwidth, and tolerance for bursty traffic. ATM Quality of Service (QoS) parameters are closely related to traffic class and traffic class parameters. Traffic class and QoS parameters combined define the traffic contract. QoS parameters include the following:

Maximum Cell Transfer Delay (CTD). The CTD is defined by calculating all network delays along the traffic's path. This QoS parameter specifies the maximum CTD acceptable.

Peak-to-Peak Cell Delay Variation (CDV). This is the amount of time variation acceptable between the arrival of cells.

Cell Loss Ratio (CLR). This is the ratio between lost cells (for any reason) and those successfully received.

Cell Error Ratio (CER). This is the ratio between cells received with errors (for any reason) and those successfully received.

We return to ATM traffic classes and QoS later when we see how the Integrated Services (IS) Internet model and the Resource Reservation Protocol (RSVP) tie in.

IP Type of Service

IP was originally meant to provide service differentiation. The Type of Service (ToS) field was intended to carry various different values indicating the different ways that packets should be treated. RFC 791, "Internet Protocol," defines the first three bits to specify something called Precedence, which could have values that translate to Network Control, Internetwork Control, Flash, Flash Override, and others. Then, three more bits act as flags to specify what your packet needs in terms of processing: maximize throughput, maximize reliability, or minimize delay. RFC 1349, "Type of Service in the Internet Protocol Suite" (now obsolete), added a fourth bit to minimize cost.

Although this is nice in theory, it didn't really work all that well in traditional internetworks, which is why the Differentiated Services (DIFF-SERV) working group got into the act. Once an IP packet is flagged for super-flash-override with ultra-low delay (I'm exaggerating, of course), it still gets shoved out of the router's back door onto an Ethernet link, where it gets treated just like any other average frame. This tends to be a problem as it negates the impact of a Type of Service field.

The other problem with ToS is that you can assure your frames always get the best service if you assign them to get the best treatment (depending on what treatment they need). Why is that a problem? Because if you *don't* assign the best treatment to your packets, because maybe they really aren't ultra urgent, then your packets are always waiting for their turn. Higher-priority packets are *always* be ahead of you, or your packets are simply dropped—after all, they didn't have very high priority, did they?

Differentiated Service

The DIFFSERV group has redefined the old IPv4 ToS field and the IPv6 Traffic Class field to be more conducive to actually providing a simple and coarse mechanism by which a few bits (two or three) of the ToS/Traffic Class fields can be used to cause forwarding routers to treat a packet appropriately. However, DIFFSERV explicitly states in its charter (see www.ietf.org/html.charters/diffserv-charter.html) that the group will not work on:

- Mechanisms for the identification of individual traffic flows
- New signaling mechanisms to support the marking of packets

- End-to-end service definitions
- Service level agreements

The Differentiated Service (DS) field (formerly Type of Service in IPv4 and Traffic Class in IPv6) is defined in RFC 2474, "Definition of the Differentiated Services Field (DS Field) in the IPv4 and IPv6 Headers." The DIFFSERV architecture is defined in RFC 2475, "An Architecture for Differentiated Services." This document defines an architecture for implementing a scalable and interoperable mechanism that allows some packets to be treated differently by forwarding routers. The differentiated services are differentiated by some "significant characteristics of packet transmission in one direction across a set of one or more paths within a network," according to RFC 2475. The characteristics must be mathematically measurable and can include throughput, delay, or some other means by which "relative priority of access to network resources" can be indicated.

According to RFC 2475, the differentiated services architecture "is composed of a number of functional elements implemented in network nodes, including a small set of per-hop forwarding behaviors, packet classification functions, and traffic conditioning functions including metering, marking, shaping, and policing." What this means is that forwarding routers do not necessarily have to keep track of traffic flows but only treat packets differently based on the DS field. Depending on the local options, a router may aggregate traffic with different DS field values, as long as they all get treated appropriately. These are called behavior aggregates, and a packet is assigned to a particular behavior aggregate as it enters a network.

With DIFFSERV, per-hop behaviors (PHBs) are defined not just by which interface a packet is routed, but also by other factors. For example, a particular DS value might indicate that the PHB should include traffic shaping, which is a mechanism by which packets are delayed so that they arrive at their destination at a particular rate of delivery. Instead, it could include metering, a mechanism by which a stream's rate is measured, or it could include policing, the dropping of packets within a metered traffic stream to make it conform to some traffic profile.

Approaches to Service Differentiation

So far, we've seen two different types of approach to service differentiation in three different incarnations. The original IP ToS field, described in RFC 791, used a relative priority model for its Precedence bits. The updated Type of Service mechanism described in RFC 1349 uses a service marking model, and the DIFFSERV approach is a refinement of this model in that each packet is marked with characteristics of the type of service desired, making it more quantitative, rather than with a more vague, relativistic value that is somehow supposed to be interpreted appropriately by forwarding routers. Instead of relying on a qualitative judgment as is done with relative priority approaches, a service marking model allows you to more easily map markings with local service levels. If a router can treat packets in only one of two ways, one of which gives maximum throughput and the other gives maximum reliability, categorizing a packet that has been marked for maximum throughput is a simple matter. It is not easy to decide in which category a packet marked "Immediate" or "Network Control" belongs.

However, there are other approaches to differentiating services. One mentioned by RFC 2474 is the label switching approach used by ATM and MPLS, discussed in Chapter 12, "IP Routing through ATM." Citing an improved granularity of control over how packets flow through the network, the RFC also notes that this comes at the cost of increased management and administrative chores necessary to distribute label switched paths.

The approach we're most interested in is the Integrated Services/RSVP model, which uses traditional datagram forwarding by default but lets communicating nodes do extra signaling to set up packet classifications and forwarding states on intermediate nodes (routers). We discuss Integrated Services (IS) and the Resource Reservation Protocol (RSVP) next.

Integrated Services and RSVP

The information RFC 1633, "Integrated Services in the Internet Architecture: an Overview," was published in 1994 and described a framework for doing more than just the traditional network applications over the Internet. The authors of RFC 1633 state: "We use the term integrated services (IS) for an Internet service model that includes best-effort service, real-time service, and controlled link sharing." In other words, the intention for IS is to provide greater control over traffic in much the same way that ATM provides traffic control. The basic goal for IS is to provide two types of services for real-time traffic— guaranteed service and predictive service—integrate them with link-sharing, and make it all work well with multicast and unicast traffic.

By guaranteed traffic, the authors of RFC 1633 mean "a service characterized by a perfectly reliable upper bound on delay." By predictive service, they mean "a fairly reliable, but not perfectly reliable, delay bound." These "guarantees" can be broadly interpreted to mean "close enough to work well enough" for real-time applications that require them. After all, Internet standards must take into consideration all the possibilities of underlying networking technologies, some of which are better suited than others to supply integrated services.

This raises one of the problems cited by IS detractors: The ubiquity of "infinite bandwidth" would make the IS approach irrelevant. There would be no reason to closely manage bandwidth if everyone has more than enough, whether via fiber optic cable in offices, cable modems to homes, satellites, or any other technology. Of course, the answer is that although it may seem that we're on the verge of effectively giving everyone as much bandwidth as they can possibly use, the truth is that bandwidth is almost certain to be distributed unevenly across the Internet into the foreseeable future.

Thus, the premise of the IS model is that bandwidth must be managed. Furthermore, IS supporters contend that mere priority (as specified in RFC 791) is not enough, as it does not do enough to differentiate between different services and fails to scale well as demand for services goes up. Likewise, the fact that applications can adapt to network environments in which traffic is delayed does not help the poor users. A video transmission might be able to recover from seconds- or even minutes-long network delays, but such delays would render the application data (perhaps an interactive video conference) unusable for the poor user.

Under the IS model, all data is processed through the same network layer protocol, usually IP. Streams would be identifiable, something not supported as part of the original Internet Protocol specification, and support for streams would have to be distributed across the entire network. The IS architecture calls for four basic components to make it work. Three of these components must be built into routers as part of a traffic control function. The traffic control components include the following:

Packet Scheduler. This component keeps track of how different packet streams are to be forwarded. Using queues, timers, or other appropriate mechanisms, the packet scheduler makes sure that packet streams are forwarded appropriately.

Classifier. This component maps each incoming packet into a class. Packets in the same class get the same type of treatment by the packet scheduler. Classes are defined locally to the router and may be as broadly or narrowly defined as desired.

Admission Control. A host or router uses the admission control component to determine whether a new flow can be permitted access with the requested QoS. Admission control implements an algorithm consistent with the service model in use.

The fourth component is a protocol that can be used to reserve resources across a network to support a particular flow. Though any number of protocols could be defined for such reservations, it is the Resource Reservation Protocol (RSVP) that is the proposed standard for this purpose. We turn to RSVP in the last part of this chapter. ATM's QoS features are well defined, and it should come as no surprise that the Integrated Services Internet, RSVP, and ATM should be closely connected.

The Integrated Services Internet and ATM

Central to the Integrated Services Internet is the concept of a resource reservation protocol. In this section, we provide an overview to the Resource Reservation Protocol (RSVP) and then summarize how it all works over ATM. There is too much material to go into all the details, but this section provides a summary and pointers to the source materials on implementing and deploying IS over RSVP and ATM.

Resource Reservation Protocol (RSVP)

In order to do Integrated Services on the Internet, we need a resource reservation protocol. The Resource ReSerVation Protocol (RSVP) is specified in proposed standard RFC 2205, "Resource ReSerVation Protocol (RSVP)—Version 1 Functional Specification." RSVP is a resource reservation setup protocol specifically designed to support an integrated services Internet as defined in RFC 1633. Hosts, as recipients of data flows or data streams from servers, can solicit specific qualities of service from the network using RSVP. Intermediate routers in paths between receiving hosts and sending hosts can use RSVP to deliver QoS requests to nodes along those paths as well as to set up and maintain the state needed to provide such service.

One sometimes controversial feature of RSVP is that it calls for maintaining state relating to data flows in intermediate routers. Traditionally, Internet protocols assume that the network does not need to be aware of specific nodes but that routers should be able to apply simple rules about forwarding packets without having to keep track of where those packets come from or whether they belong to some particular flow of packets.

RSVP works in one direction: from the receiving host to the sending host. It operates just over IP, parallel to transport protocols such as UDP and TCP, but it behaves more like an Internet control protocol such as routing protocols. However, it is not a routing protocol, even though it depends on routing protocols to obtain routes between nodes.

The RSVP mechanism operates very much like that described in RFC 1633 (and above), with components to do packet scheduling, classifying, and admission control. The policy control function is used to determine whether the user is permitted to set up the reservation. The admission control function is used to determine whether the resources are available.

Figure 13.1, taken from RFC 2205, shows how RSVP is implemented in hosts and routers. As it demonstrates, RSVP happens in parallel to the flow of data, and it controls the flow of data so that it conforms to the quality of service and resource reservation parameters that were initially set up.

RSVP supports both unicast and multicast. Resource reservation for multicasts can present problems, especially if the reservations must be done by the sending host. With RSVP, recipient hosts take care of the reservations, easing the problem for the sender.

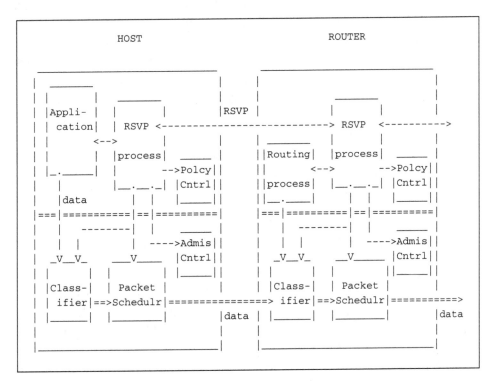

Figure 13.1 RSVP in hosts and routers (from RFC 2205).

RSVP reservation requests contain a flowspec and a filter spec. Together, these are referred to as a flow descriptor. The flowspec indicates the quality of service desired for the session and is used to determine how the data is handled at the link layer. In other words, it defines how the data packets are treated by the host. The flowspec consists of a service class, a definition of the desired QoS, and a value describing the data flow. Although RSVP passes this information from node to node, it does not do anything with it directly. The type and representation of data within the flowspec are specified as part of the integrated services model rather than as part of RSVP. RFV 2210, "The Use of RSVP with IETF Integrated Services," is the proposed standard specification that defines how this works.

The filter spec specifies how packets are to be classified, including whether or not they belong to a particular flow, and if so, which flow they belong to. The contents of the filter specs can vary depending on whether IPv4 or IPv6 is being used; they may consist simply of sets of IP addresses and port numbers or use other fields in the IP headers.

The way RSVP works is that a receiving host initiates an RSVP message, sending the message "upstream" to the sending host. When an intermediate node (router) gets the RSVP request, it checks the request against the admission control and the policy control. If the requesting user has sufficient privilege to request the reservation and the resource is available, then two things happen. First, the intermediate node makes a reservation for the requesting node on its own link. Second, the intermediate node forwards the request upstream to the next intermediate node in the data path where the process begins again.

When multicast data paths converge (as shown in Figure 13.2), the node at which the paths converge is required to merge the reservations together. This minimizes the resources necessary to support multicasts because only one reservation is necessary between any two nodes, even if the downstream node serves more than one other node beyond itself.

RSVP, Integrated Services, and ATM

Four separate RFCs document the issues involved in implementing RSVP and Integrated Services over ATM. The problem and solution are discussed in a general way in informational RFC 2382, "A Framework for Integrated Services and RSVP over ATM." This RFC compares and contrasts the traditional best-effort IP delivery model with the Integrated Services model and discusses how QoS and traffic class parameters and functions can best be mapped from IP to ATM.

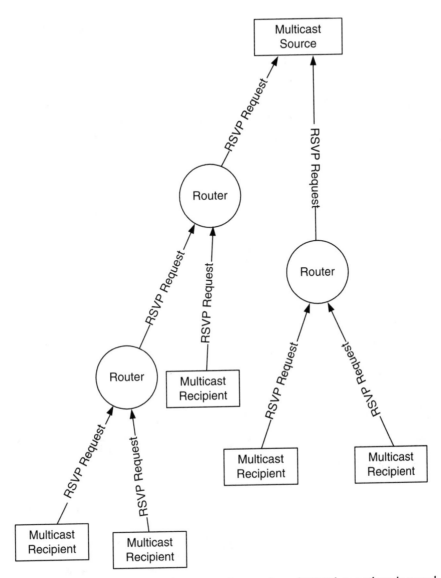

Figure 13.2   As multicast paths merge, the number of RSVP interactions is pared.

Proposed standard RFC 2380, "RSVP over ATM Implementation Requirements," discusses the basic requirements necessary to implement RSVP over ATM. In particular, it provides guidelines for how RSVP uses ATM virtual circuits to make connections and how to support multicast RSVP sessions.

Another proposed standard, RFC 2381, "Interoperation of Controlled-Load Service and Guaranteed Service with ATM," discusses approaches to mapping service classes and traffic management mechanisms between

IP and ATM. This specification describes how IP guaranteed quality of service (RFC 2212, "Specification of Guaranteed Quality of Service") and controlled load service (RFC 2211, "Specification of the Controlled-Load Network Element Service") can be mapped onto ATM traffic classes and quality of service parameters.

Finally, RFC 2379, "RSVP over ATM Implementation Guidelines," provides implementation guidelines for running RSVP over ATM SVCs. RFC 2379 is a Best Current Practice document (BCP 24) and provides guidelines for using ATM virtual circuits to carry RSVP messages.

Reading List

Table 13.1 lists many of the RFCs that address quality of service, resource reservation, integrated and differentiated services over the Internet, and ATM. Defining tools that allow transmission of real-time applications over the Internet is a very complex pursuit. Work is far from over in this direction, and the interested reader should use these documents as starting points for learning more about particular aspects of traffic management issues.

Table 13.1   RFCs about Quality of Service, Resource Reservation, and ATM

RFC	STATUS	TITLE
RFC 1633	Informational	Integrated Services in the Internet Architecture: an Overview
RFC 1821	Informational	Integration of Real-time Services in an IP-ATM Network Architecture
RFC 1889	Proposed Std.	RTP: A Transport Protocol for Real-Time Applications
RFC 2205	Proposed Std.	Resource ReSerVation Protocol (RSVP)—Version 1 Functional Specification
RFC 2210	Proposed Std.	The Use of RSVP with IETF Integrated Services
RFC 2211	Proposed Std.	Specification of the Controlled-Load Network Element Service
RFC 2212	Proposed Std.	Specification of Guaranteed Quality of Service
RFC 2215	Proposed Std.	General Characterization Parameters for Integrated Service Network Elements
RFC 2216	Informational	Network Element Service Specification Template

Table 13.1   *(Continued)*

RFC	STATUS	TITLE
RFC 2379	BCP 24	RSVP over ATM Implementation Guidelines
RFC 2380	Proposed Std.	RSVP over ATM Implementation Requirements
RFC 2381	Proposed Std.	Interoperation of Controlled-Load Service and Guaranteed Service with ATM
RFC 2382	Informational	A Framework for Integrated Services and RSVP over ATM
RFC 2386	Informational	A Framework for QoS-based Routing in the Internet
RFC 2474	Proposed Std.	Definition of the Differentiated Services Field (DS Field) in the IPv4 and IPv6 Headers
RFC 2475	Informational	An Architecture for Differentiated Services
RFC 2502	Informational	Limitations of Internet Protocol Suite for Distributed Simulation the Large Multicast Environment

ATM Management

In this chapter, we look at ATM management issues covered by Internet standards. Very broadly, these can be characterized as belonging to one of two categories: those specifications that relate to the Integrated Local Management Interface (ILMI) and those that define managed objects and MIBs related to ATM.

We've already discussed Internet standards for network management in Chapter 7. After taking a brief look at the ILMI standard from the ATM Forum and how it is applied to ATMARP, MARS, and NHRP, we summarize the standards work done on ATM-related managed objects and MIBs.

Integrated Local Management Interface

The ATM Forum defined the Integrated Local Management Interface (ILMI) to provide a mechanism by which ATM management systems can exchange SNMPv1 information directly. In other words, every ATM device—from an ATM workstation to ATM network switches to ATM routers—contains an SNMP agent application and an SNMP management application. When queried by another ATM device, the agent provides requested information; when the device needs information from another system, the management application requests it.

Because ILMI allows ATM systems to exchange network management information without resorting to IP, it is useful for enabling systems to access ATM-level services such as ATMARP, MARS, and NHRP.

The ATM Forum's ILMI Specification

ILMI is used for the exchange of ATM interface parameters. The ATM Forum ILMI specification describes four different ATM interface MIB modules. They include:

- The Textual Conventions MIB specifies how objects are identified as well as other textual conventions relating to the data contained in the other MIBs.

- The Link Management MIB is used to manage ATM interface links.

- The Address Registration MIB is used to register ATM addresses for the User Network Interface (UNI).

- The Service Registry MIB is used to keep track of ATM network services (for example, LAN Emulation Configuration Servers [LECSs]).

ILMI supports basic SNMP commands for retrieving information from SNMP agents (get and get-next), as well as the ability to rewrite data (set) and send out notifications of extraordinary events (traps). To avoid confusion, the ILMI standard defines the switch end of a circuit as the "network side," while the host or router end of the circuit is treated as the "user side." Using this convention, the Service Registry MIB always receives queries from the user side (the host or router) while always implementing the Service Registry MIB on the network side (the switch).

Of particular interest for Internet specifications is the Service Registry MIB, because ATM switches are required to support this MIB if they support IP over ATM. This is how a row in the Service Registry MIB is defined, using ASN.1 notation (taken from RFC 2601):

```
AtmfSrvcRegEntry ::= SEQUENCE {
    atmfSrvcRegPort          INTEGER,
```

```
atmfSrvcRegServiceID      OBJECT IDENTIFIER,
atmfSrvcRegATMAddress     AtmAddress,
atmfSrvcRegAddressIndex   INTEGER,
atmfSrvcRegParm1          OCTET STRING
}
```

Table 14.1, adapted from RFC 2601, defines the fields in this structure.

Using the Service Registry MIB, switches (the "network side" of a circuit) can be queried by hosts and routers (the "user side" of the circuit) for information about services available on the network. Since the queries and responses use SNMP version 1, which is quite simple and widely implemented, it becomes a simple matter to advertise various services in this way. Since the SNMP queries and responses are carried directly over ATM, stations can bypass IP issues to get the information they need to use IP over ATM.

Internet Standards Using ILMI

The three proposed standard RFCs that define ILMI-based server discovery are listed in Table 14.2. Each of these specifications is very brief and to the point, describing ILMI in two paragraphs, listing the ASN.1 definition of the Service Registry MIB table entries, and then detailing how ILMI-based server discovery works for ATMARP, MARS, and NHRP servers.

Table 14.1 Fields in a Service Registry MIB Row (from RFC 2601)

FIELD NAME	DEFINITION
AtmfSrvcRegPort	The ATM port number for which this entry contains management information. The value of zero may be used to indicate the ATM interface over which a management request was received.
AtmfSrvcRegServiceID	This service identifier uniquely identifies the type of service at the address provided in the table.
AtmfSrvcRegATMAddress	This is the full address of the service. The ATM client uses this address to establish a connection with the service.
AtmfSrvcRegAddressIndex	An arbitrary integer to differentiate multiple rows containing different ATM addresses for the same service on the same port.
AtmfSrvcRegParm1	An octet string whose size and meaning is determined by the value of atmfSrvcRegServiceID.

Table 14.2   ILMI-Based Server Discovery RFCs

RFC	TITLE
RFC 2601	ILMI-Based Server Discovery for ATMARP
RFC 2602	ILMI-Based Server Discovery for MARS
RFC 2603	ILMI-Based Server Discovery for NHRP

In each of these three specifications, a service parameter string is defined for the service registry table that allows protocol-specific parameters to be indicated. Each RFC also specifies a service object identifier to name the service being described in the MIB, and each RFC specifies client and server behavior. Suffice it to say that RFC 2601, "ILMI-Based Server Discovery for ATMARP," remains consistent with the specification that defines ATMARP, RFC 2225, "Classical IP and ARP over ATM." RFC 2601 (MARS) remains consistent with the specification for MARS (RFC 2022, "Support for Multicast over UNI 3.0/3.1 based ATM Networks"). RFC 2603 (NHRP) remains consistent with the specification for NHRP (RFC 2332, "NBMA Next Hop Resolution Protocol").

Managed Objects and MIBs

MIB and managed objects specifications tend to be quite long, if only because they must reproduce lengthy ASN.1 definitions. Rather than attempting to provide all the details of every MIB, in this section we briefly introduce some of the MIB and managed objects relevant to ATM networks.

Managed Objects for ATM Management

The basic specification for ATM management is contained in proposed standard RFC 2515, "Definitions of Managed Objects for ATM Management." An ATM management object is used for tasks such as managing ATM interfaces, virtual links, and AAL5 entities and connections supported by ATM hosts, switches, and networks. RFC 2515 is concerned mostly with ATM PVCs rather than SVCs; although it does include some SVC management information, SVC management can sometimes be complex and requires special attention such as that provided under the Interface Group MIB (see next section). RFC 2515 is necessary, but not sufficient to manage all ATM interfaces, links, and cross-connects. For example, the basic MIB-II (RFC 1213, STD 17, "Management Information Base for Network Management of TCP/IP-based Internets—MIB-II") is required of all systems; other MIBs relating to applications that use ATM may also be required.

RFC 2515 arranges ATM managed objects into different tables, summarized below (taken from RFC 2515):

ATM interface configuration table. This table contains information on ATM cell layer configuration of local ATM interfaces on an ATM device in addition to the information on such interfaces contained in the ifTable (interface table).

ATM interface DS3 PLCP and TC sublayer tables. These tables provide performance statistics of the DS3 (Digital Signal Level 3, equivalent to a T-3 communication link) Physical Layer Convergence Protocol (PLCP) and transmission convergence (TC) sublayer of local ATM interfaces on a managed ATM device. DS3 PLCP and TC sublayer are currently used to carry ATM cells, respectively, over DS3 and SONET transmission paths.

ATM traffic parameter table.

ATM interface virtual link (VPL/VCL) configuration tables. The ATM virtual link tables are used to create, delete, or modify ATM virtual links in an ATM host, ATM switch, and ATM network. ATM virtual link tables along with the cross-connect tables are used to create, delete, or modify ATM cross-connects in an ATM switch or ATM network (for example, for customer network management purposes).

ATM VP/VC cross-connect tables. The ATM switch and ATM network implement the ATM VP/VC cross-connect tables in a carrier's network for Customer Network Management (CNM) purposes.

AAL5 connection performance statistics table. This is used to provide AAL5 performance information for each AAL5 virtual connection that is terminated at the AAL5 entity contained within an ATM switch or host.

In addition to providing complete ASN.1 definitions, RFC 2515 explains how the MIB it defines interacts and fits in with other MIBs, such as the System Group of MIB-II and the Interface Group.

The Interfaces Group MIB

It is a convenience to be able to talk about IP being the network layer protocol that sits on top of some monolithic link layer protocol, but it is not always correct. The proposed standard RFC 2233, "The Interfaces Group MIB Using SMIv2," documents mechanisms for representing more complicated interface situations and for storing and manipulating management data relating to these situations.

Complications in the interfaces table of MIB-II arise from a number of areas. First, some link layer technologies use sublayers, such as ATM. Should interface management information be limited to the ATM Adaptation Layer, or should a separate interface entry be added to a table for each virtual circuit associated with a station? Another issue is the difference between link layer technologies: Ethernet frames are relatively simple to count and measure, but is it more appropriate to keep track of ATM cells or ATM protocol data units? Or both? The Interfaces Group MIB spells out an approach to mapping complex interfaces onto a usable network management schema.

The IP over ATM MIB

RFC 2320, "Definitions of Managed Objects for Classical IP and ARP over ATM Using SMIv2 (IPOA-MIB)," is a proposed standard for IPOA management information. It creates an MIB structure that consists of three parts. First, the Basic Support MIB definitions must be supported by any IP and ARP over ATM entities (clients and ATMARP servers). Second, the Client Supported MIB definitions must be supported by clients. Third, the Server Supported MIB definitions must be supported by any servers (ATMARP servers). The modeling of ATM layers defined in RFC 2515 is assumed as a prerequisite for the IPOA MIB.

Clients and ATMARP servers must both implement the basic support, consisting of the following:

- An ATM Logical IP subnet (LIS) table that indicates the subnets to which the system belongs.

- An ATM Logical IP Subnet interface mapping table, for mapping an LIS to each ATM interface. A switch might have multiple subnets mapped to the same ATM interface; most clients map only a single subnet to any individual interface.

- An ATMARP remote server table contains an entry for ATMARP server(s) for each logical IP subnet and ATM interface.

- An ATM VC table contains entries for each virtual circuit linking an ATM interface to a destination IP address.

- An ATM config PVC table contains entries based on Inverse ATMARP replies, reflecting the IP address of stations at the other end of PVCs.

- Support for a notification object is required, indicating that a maximum transmission unit (MTU) has been exceeded.

In addition to the basic support listed above, clients must also support an ATMARP client table to map IP addresses to ATM addresses, as well as to support various ARP-related functions. ATMARP servers are required to support an ATMARP server table, listing all the ATMARP servers within an LIS. They must also support additional notifications to report the existence of a duplicate IP address and the creation or deletion of a logical IP subnet.

Textual Conventions for MIB Modules

The SMI (discussed in Chapter 7, "Network Management Fundamentals") defines many object identifiers, but sometimes new ones are necessary. RFC 2514, "Definitions of Textual Conventions and OBJECT-IDENTITIES for ATM Management," is a proposed standard for describing textual conventions (according to RFC 1903, "Textual Conventions for Version 2 of the Simple Network Management Protocol (SNMPv2)," new types are called "textual conventions"). RFC 2514 defines objects such as AtmAddr, which represents an ATM address whose semantics are implied by the length of the value. It also defines AtmServiceCategory, which indicates the service category of a connection, and other objects relevant to ATM networking.

Accounting Information for ATM Networks

According to the proposed standard RFC 2513, "Managed Objects for Controlling the Collection and Storage of Accounting Information for Connection-Oriented Networks," it is useful in some networks for network managers to keep track of who is using bandwidth and network resources. For example, in ATM networks, it is worthwhile keeping track of who is using VCs. Collecting such accounting data through SNMP, by gathering ATM connection information from every station all the time, means moving a great deal of information across the network.

Because moving such volumes of information a little bit at a time over SNMP is not economically sustainable, the alternative is to have stations collect and store that information in files, which may be retrieved in bulk when it is convenient.

RFC 2513 defines a model in which ATM switches collect data about their connections and store them in files. One file might be used for PVCs and another for SVCs. Using different files allows the collection of different types of information for different uses. When administrators are ready to collect the data, they notify the switch to stop storing data into that file (and start putting new data into another file). Administrators can then retrieve the closed file using an efficient file transfer mechanism.

RFC 2513 defines the format and mechanisms for collecting such data as well as the mechanisms by which an administrator defines what data is to be collected. RFC 2512, "Accounting Information for ATM Networks," defines a subtree that holds a set of objects that define the accounting information applicable to ATM connections.

Reading List

Table 14.3 lists RFCs that describe network management issues pertaining to ATM. Another important resource for this chapter is the ATM Forum specification for ILMI, "Integrated Local Management Interface (ILMI) Specification Version 4.0." A Portable Data Format (.pdf) version of this document can be found at:

```
ftp://ftp.atmforum.com/pub/approved-specs/af-ilmi-0065.000.pdf
```

Other versions of the document are available on the ATM Forum ftp site, at:

```
ftp://ftp.atmforum.com/pub/approved-specs/
```

RFCs cited in the reading list for Chapter 7 are also helpful for understanding the MIB and managed object issues discussed in this chapter.

Table 14.3   ATM Management RFCs

RFC	STATUS	TITLE
RFC 2011	Proposed Std.	SNMPv2 Management Information Base for the Internet Protocol Using SMIv2
RFC 2233	Proposed Std.	The Interfaces Group MIB Using SMIv2

Table 14.3 (Continued)

RFC	STATUS	TITLE
RFC 2320	Proposed Std.	Definitions of Managed Objects for Classical IP and ARP over ATM Using SMIv2 (IPOA-MIB)
RFC 2512	Proposed Std.	Accounting Information for ATM Networks
RFC 2513	Proposed Std.	Managed Objects for Controlling the Collection and Storage of Accounting Information for Connection-Oriented Networks
RFC 2514	Proposed Std.	Definitions of Textual Conventions and OBJECT-IDENTITIES for ATM Management
RFC 2515	Proposed Std.	Definitions of Managed Objects for ATM Management
RFC 2558	Proposed Std.	Definitions of Managed Objects for the SONET/SDH Interface Type
RFC 2601	Proposed Std.	ILMI-Based Server Discovery for ATMARP
RFC 2602	Proposed Std.	ILMI-Based Server Discovery for MARS
RFC 2603	Proposed Std.	ILMI-Based Server Discovery for NHRP

The Future of ATM and IP

In this chapter, we look ahead to future developments in ATM and related Internet standards. In addition to looking at the works in progress of the various IETF groups working on ATM-related issues, we start this chapter with a look at IPv6 over ATM. IPv6 is already here, and the specifications for running IPv6 over ATM are also already specified as proposed standards. However, as of the mid 1999, only a handful of products support IPv6, and only two service providers (one in Australia and one in Argentina) have announced IPv6 services. Even though the standards have been proposed, experimentation with the new version of IP is ongoing.

Unlike network applications, which can catch on very quickly, progress in defining how lower-layer technologies work together is much slower. There is only a minimal barrier to testing, deploying, or implementing a new application—just install it on a personal computer connected to a network.. The barriers to trying out something new at the link layer are much higher: Instead of an application on one or two systems, the entire infrastructure for at least one network must be changed. That can mean new cabling, new network interfaces, new switches, bridges, routers, and other forwarding or repeating devices, as well as new software. As we see in the summaries of workgroup activities, progress in the IP over ATM field is incremental and evolutionary.

After introducing the relevant specifications for IPv6 over ATM, we look at the activities of several workgroups relevant to ATM. These include the Multiprotocol Label Switching workgroup (mpls), chartered to specify label switching and forwarding standards; the Integrated Services workgroup (intserv), chartered to come up with the minimal requirements necessary to turn the Internet into a platform for carrying real-time applications; and the AToM MIB workgroup (atom-mib), chartered to review the proposed standard for managed objects for ATM.

IPv6 over ATM

Two proposed standards specify how IPv6 is to work over ATM. RFC 2491, "IPv6 over Non-Broadcast Multiple Access (NBMA) Networks," describes in detail how IPv6 works over nonbroadcast multiaccess (NBMA) networks. The detail is generalized, however, because one of the design goals of IPv6 was to move away from dealing directly with link layer protocols and generalize the protocol so that any link layer protocol could be supported. IPv6 inherently presumes that the link layer protocol is capable of doing multicast, natively. With ATM, multicast requires some added mechanism.

Why is multicast necessary? Because to avoid getting involved with interfacing to link layers for IP address resolution purposes, IPv6 mandates neighbor discovery (ND). Proposed standard RFC 2461, "Neighbor Discovery for IP Version 6 (IPv6)," describes how ND works and what it does. In a nutshell, the purpose is to allow nodes on any network to use multicast to locate servers, routers, and other "neighbors" on the local link—all without getting the network layer (IP) involved. Of course, this can present a problem for NBMA networks like ATM where multicast is not natively defined but rather is implemented through some mechanism that simulates the multicast function. In fact, RFC 2491 indicates that the MARS architecture should be used to provide that simulated multicast function in IPv6 over NBMA networks.

RFC 2491 (along with RFC 2461) explains how IPv6 works over any NBMA network and covers the most important issues and solutions.

RFC 2492, "IPv6 over ATM Networks," is also a proposed standard, but it provides the more specific technical solutions relevant directly for ATM networks. This document details how encapsulations are done for IPv6 over ATM as well as specifying how MARS, NHRP, and ND control messages are to be formatted.

One of the features of IPv6 is that network addresses are much easier to generate and are usually generated for a node from that node's own interface address. The interface address procedures by default expect a 48-bit value because that is the size of most LAN interface addresses. In ATM networks, stations may have an ATM End System Address (AESA), or may have been assigned a 48-bit MAC address, or may have a 64-bit EUI address value (a global value based on an IEEE standard for link layer addressing), or even an E.164 address. Each of these values can be used as an interface token from which a valid IPv6 address can be formed. RFC 2492 discusses how these different interface tokens are used.

Multiprotocol Label Switching Working Group (mpls)

As we saw in Chapter 12, "IP Routing through ATM," Multiprotocol Label Switching defines an important technology for forwarding cells through an ATM network. Early on, many vendors seized this approach, and work on refining and defining the specifications continues. The mpls working group has published many Internet-Drafts, listed in Table 15.1, but as of mid 1999 none had been published as RFCs.

The mpls group is chartered to standardize the base technology for the label swapping forwarding model (label switching). This includes building a standard for the way in which label switching is used with network layer routing as well as defining standards for using label switching over various different link layer network technologies such as ATM, Ethernet, Frame Relay, Token Ring, and any others that might be appropriate.

The group's tasks include defining protocols for distributing labels among routers, for implementing multicast, for supporting resource reservations as well as quality of service mechanisms, and for defining appropriate behaviors for hosts using label switching.

Table 15.1 MPLS Working Group Internet-Drafts

TITLE
A Framework for Multiprotocol Label Switching
Use of Label Switching With RSVP
Multiprotocol Label Switching Architecture
MPLS Label Stack Encoding
The Assignment of the Information Field and Protocol Identifier in the Q.2941 Generic Identifier and Q.2957 User-to-user Signaling for the Internet Protocol
Use of Label Switching on Frame Relay Networks Specification
VCID Notification over ATM link
Carrying Label Information in BGP-4
Requirements for Traffic Engineering Over MPLS
LDP Specification
Definitions of Managed Objects for the Multiprotocol Label Switching, Label Distribution Protocol (LDP)
MPLS using ATM VC Switching
LDP State Machine
Extensions to RSVP for LSP Tunnels
Constraint-Based LSP Setup using LDP
MPLS Traffic Engineering Management Information Base Using SMIv2
MPLS Capability set
Explicit Tree Routing
MPLS Support of Differentiated Services by ATM LSRs and Frame Relay LSRs
MPLS Loop Prevention Mechanism
Framework for IP Multicast in MPLS
MPLS Label Switch Router Management Information Base Using SMIv2

Integrated Services (intserv)

As we saw in Chapter 13, "Managing Network Traffic," advancing the type of application that is possible over the Internet requires building a new model for internetworking, which includes quality of service as well as resource reservation. Real-time applications just won't work very well unless they can be given service guarantees, and the Integrated Services (intserv) working group is focused on three problems in this area:

- Defining the problem. The intserv group must first define the Integrated Services Internet model.

- Building interfaces that allow an application to express its end-to-end requirements for service guarantees that define what information is available to individual routers in the network and that specify what (if any) additional expectations the service model can make on link layer technologies.

- Developing a set of requirements that enable routers to make certain that the appropriate service levels can be delivered to applications and that the Internet can support the integrated services model.

Currently, the group has published several RFCs, listed in Table 15.2. They are still doing work in the area of IP flows that has been documented in Internet-Drafts.

Table 15.2 Integrated Services Working Group RFCs

RFC	STATUS	TITLE
RFC 2210	Proposed Std.	The Use of RSVP with IETF Integrated Services
RFC 2211	Proposed Std.	Specification of the Controlled-Load Network Element Service
RFC 2212	Proposed Std.	Specification of Guaranteed Quality of Service
RFC 2213	Proposed Std.	Integrated Services Management Information Base using SMIv2
RFC 2214	Proposed Std.	Integrated Services Management Information Base Guaranteed Service Extensions using SMIv2
RFC 2215	Proposed Std.	General Characterization Parameters for Integrated Service Network Elements
RFC 2216	Informational	Network Element Service Specification Template

AToM MIB (atommib)

The AToM MIB Working Group was originally chartered to evaluate RFC 1695, "Definitions of Managed Objects for ATM Management Version 8.0 using SMIv2," which has been made obsolete by the publication of RFC 2515 (discussed in Chapter 14, "ATM Management"). This group is also responsible for defining additional sets of managed objects to be used for managing ATM services, testing, and for the frame based UNI (user-network interface). Table 15.3 lists the RFCs published by the group.

Reading List

The best place to find the latest information about working group activities is the Active IETF Working Groups page, at www.ietf.org/html.charters/wg-dir.html.

New working groups are formed periodically when new needs are identified and existing ones close down when they have fulfilled their chartered goals (or, occasionally, for lack of interest or because their work loses relevance). Table 15.4 lists the working groups whose work currently is most relevant to ATM issues and URLs pointing to their charter pages.

The ATM Forum is another good resource for information about the future directions of ATM. The Web site is www.atmforum.com/.

Table 15.3   AToM MIB Working Group RFCs

RFC	STATUS	TITLE
RFC 1595	Obsolete	Definitions of Managed Objects for the SONET/SDH Interface Type
RFC 2493	Proposed Std.	Textual Conventions for MIB Modules Using Performance History Based on 15 Minute Intervals
RFC 2512	Proposed Std.	Accounting Information for ATM Networks
RFC 2513	Proposed Std.	Managed Objects for Controlling the Collection and Storage of Accounting Information for Connection-Oriented Networks
RFC 2514	Proposed Std.	Definitions of Textual Conventions and OBJECT-IDENTITIES for ATM Management
RFC 2515	Proposed Std.	Definitions of Managed Objects for ATM Management
RFC 2558	Proposed Std.	Definitions of Managed Objects for the SONET/SDH Interface Type

Table 15.4   IETF Working Groups Pursuing ATM-Related Issues

WORKING GROUP NAME	URL
AToM MIB (atommib)	www.ietf.org/html.charters/atommib-charter.html
Multiprotocol Label Switching (MPLS)	www.ietf.org/html.charters/mpls-charter.html
Integrated Services (intserv)	www.ietf.org/html.charters/intserv-charter.html

Using the Companion CD-ROM

The companion CD-ROM contains the complete text of this book in a fully searchable, digital format. The PDF file contains a hyperlink to each of the RFCs and protocols discussed in the text. Just click on the link and access the RFC or protocol directly from the rfc-editor.org site.

What You Need

In order to use the CD-ROM, you'll need:

- IBM compatible running Windows 3.1 or better, or a Mac running OS 7.0 or better
- 16 MB RAM
- Web browser installed
- Internet connection
- Adobe Acrobat Reader 4.0
- 4MG of space on your hard drive (if you plan to install Adobe Acrobat Reader from the CD-ROM)

The Adobe Acrobat Reader 4.0 for 16 bit, 32 bit, and Mac operating systems are included on the CD-ROM in the Reader directory. To install it on your computer, open the subfolder for your operating system, and double click on the installation file.

Accessing the RFCs

The PDF file contains hyperlinks to the RFCs and Protocols discussed in the book. To access the text:

Double-click on the file email.pdf that is located in the root directory. This launches Adobe Acrobat Reader and opens the searchable version of the text. If you prefer, you can open email.pdf directly from the File menu in Adobe Acrobat Reader. Choose Open, and access your CD-ROM drive to browse for the email.pdf file.

Accessing the RFCs and protocols is easy. Just click on the hyperlink for the RFC or protocol you want to access. Adobe Acrobat will launch your Web browser and bring up the current version of the file you selected.

NOTE To take advantage of the hyperlink feature, you may need to configure Adobe Acrobat Reader to recognize your browser. If your browser does not launch when you click on a hyperlink:

1. In the File menu of Adobe Acrobat Reader, choose Preferences and select Weblink. The Weblink Preferences window appears.

2. In the textbox under Web Browser Application, enter the path to your browser. If you do not know the path, click the browse button to locate the application on your computer. Select the application file and click the OK button. The path is inserted into the text box.

3. Connection Type, select the name of your browser from the drop-down menu.

4. Click OK to save your selections.

User Assistance and Information

The software accompanying this book is being provided as is without warranty or support of any kind. Should you require basic installation assistance, or if your media is defective, please call our product support number at (212) 850-6194 weekdays between 9 am and 4 pm Eastern Standard Time. Or, we can be reached via e-mail at: wprtusw@wiley.com.

To place additional orders or to request information about other Wiley products, please call (800) 879-4539.

Index